# Group coaching for entrepreneurial learning

Lachlan Schaffer

Abstract

The challenges of entrepreneurship make learning integral to the entrepreneurial process. However, many entrepreneurs work in relative isolation and lack opportunities to engage with peers in ways that promote meaningful reflection and learning. This study explores the experience of group coaching as a setting for meaningful learning and change in entrepreneurs. Scholars studying similar group settings have shown that social processes, including those related to peer learning and identity work, contribute to entrepreneurial learning (EL) and identity construction in important ways. Still, relatively little is known about how these social processes unfold or about the different types of social contexts in which EL occurs. This study advances the literature through a narrative exploration of eight entrepreneurs' experiences navigating challenges related to entrepreneurial learning and identity in the social context of their coaching groups.

Data collection was accomplished via one-on-one, semi-structured narrative interviews with each participant. The data were interpreted using separate and sequential narrative/performative and thematic analytical methods to produce an in-depth, multidimensional understanding of the data. Participants' stories depicted group coaching as a viable context for supporting entrepreneurial learning and change on multiple levels. In addition, the study findings contribute to an understanding of *where* or *under what conditions* EL unfolds within group coaching, and *how* or *in what ways* participant entrepreneurs experience learning in this context.  Finally, the relational context of the interview itself was

found to contribute to participants' meaning making, directly influencing their constructions

of past events and their meaning.  The study presents practical implications for coaches,

coaching educators, and entrepreneurs, as well as recommendations for future research.


KEYWORDS: ENTREPRENEURSHIP, ENTREPRENEURIAL LEARNING,

ENTREPRENEURIAL IDENTITY, IDENTITY DEVELOPMENT, COACHING, GROUP

COACHING, CRITICAL REFLECTION, EXPERIENTIAL LEARNING, SOCIAL

LEARNING, NARRATIVE INQUIRY, NARRATIVE ANALYSIS.

Table of Contents


CHAPTER ONE: INTRODUCTION ------------------------------------------------1

Personal Interest in This Topic ------------------------------------------1

A Case Example from Practice --------------------------------------------3

Overview -----------------------------------------------------------------5

CHAPTER TWO: LITERATURE REVIEW ------------------------------------6

Entrepreneurship ---------------------------------------------------------7

Challenges Inherent in Entrepreneurship ----------------------------8

Entrepreneurial Learning ----------------------------------------------- 14

Experiential Learning Perspectives ----------------------------- 16

Organizational Learning Perspectives -------------------------- 23

Social/Contextual Learning Perspectives ----------------------- 28

Learning and Entrepreneurial Identity ---------------------------------- 37

Linking EL and Identity --------------------------------------- 38

Construction of Entrepreneurial Identity ------------------------ 39

Discursive Resources and Identity Construction --------------------- 41

Conclusions from the Entrepreneurship Literature ---------------------- 47

Learning how to Learn from Experience ------------------------- 47

Learning with and from Other Entrepreneurs ---------------------- 49

Constructing and Negotiating Entrepreneurial Identity ------------------ 51

Group Coaching ------------------------------------------------------- 52

Group Coaching: Definition and Context ------------------------ 53

Group-Based Learning and Change Mechanisms ------------------------ 59

Participant Narratives in Group Coaching Research ---------------------- 70

Conclusions from the Group Coaching Literature ---------------------------------- 72

Conclusion of Chapter 2 --------------------------------------------------- 74

Focus and Significance of the Inquiry ----------------------------------------- 74

CHAPTER THREE: METHODS --------------------------------------------- 77

Research Design ----------------------------------------------------------- 77

Purpose and Research Question --------------------------------------- 77

Research Approach ----------------------------------------------------- 77

Design ------------------------------------------------------------------ 90

Protection of Human Participants ----------------------------------------105

Researcher Statement ---------------------------------------------------106

Pilot Study ----------------------------------------------------------------110

Summary ----------------------------------------------------------------115

CHAPTER FOUR: FINDINGS --------------------------------------------------116

Part 1: Conditions ----------------------------------------------------------118

Social Environment ----------------------------------------------------------118

Social Processes ----------------------------------------------------------124

The Coach's Presence ----------------------------------------------------135

Conclusion of Part 1 ----------------------------------------------------138

Part 2: Process Moves ----------------------------------------------------139

Learning Vicariously ----------------------------------------------------139

Learning Through Feedback ----------------------------------------------149

Counter-Narratives ------------------------------------------------------------161

Conditions and Process Moves: A Tentative Connection ----------------165

Conclusion of Part 2 ----------------------------------------------------------166

Part 3: Relational Context of the Interview -----------------------------------168

Discursive Performances ------------------------------------------------169

Conclusion of Part 3 ----------------------------------------------------176

Conclusion of Chapter 4 ------------------------------------------------------176

Conditions ----------------------------------------------------------------177

Process Moves -----------------------------------------------------------180

Relational Context of the Interview --------------------------------------182

CHAPTER FIVE: DISCUSSION -----------------------------------------------183

Contributions to Literature -----------------------------------------------------184

Group Coaching Supports EL ------------------------------------------185

Conditions Needed to Achieve EL -----------------------------------------189

Different Processes of Learning and Change ----------------------------193

The Research Process as a Continuation of the Coaching Experience -202

Limitations ---------------------------------------------------------------------205

Recommendations for Future Research --------------------------------------207

Entrepreneurship Research ----------------------------------------------207

Coaching Research -------------------------------------------------------208

Implications for Practice -------------------------------------------------------209

Coaching ------------------------------------------------------------------210

Entrepreneurship ---------------------------------------------------------212

Conclusion ------------------------------------------------------------------------213

List of Tables

Table 1: Unaffiliated Group vs. Work Team Coaching ----------------------------------- 58

Table 2: Prominent Approaches in Group Coaching ---------------------------------------- 61

Table 3: Description of the Participants ------------------------------------------------------ 96

Table 4: Background Conditions --------------------------------------------------------------179

Table 5: Typology of Process Moves --------------------------------------------------------181

## CHAPTER ONE: INTRODUCTION

The purpose of this study was to explore the experience of group coaching as a setting for entrepreneurial learning (EL) and change.  Although research on EL has expanded over the past decade, little is known about the social processes involved in EL and the different types of social contexts in which EL occurs (Wang & Chugh, 2014).  Group coaching, meanwhile, has received scarce attention from researchers despite a surge in the commercial popularity of group-based coaching formats.  The present study advances these literatures through a narrative exploration of eight entrepreneurs' experiences participating in group coaching.  Specifically, this study explored individual entrepreneurs' experiences bringing issues and challenges they might otherwise engage with in isolation into a group coaching setting—a phenomenon I defined as "coming in from the cold."  The study used a narrative approach to investigate the meaning entrepreneurs make of their experiences navigating learning-related challenges in the social context of their coaching groups.

The expression, "coming in from the cold" refers to the act of joining or rejoining a group or society after having been separated or excluded from it in some way.  British author John le Carré helped popularize the term in his 1963 spy novel, *The Spy Who Came in From the Cold*.  In it, the protagonist longs to abandon the morally corrupt work of Cold War espionage, but is asked to "stay in the cold" for one last mission.  In the context of this study, coming in from the cold refers to the entrepreneurial journey out of isolation and loneliness and into a peer learning environment facilitated by a professionally trained coach.  Coaching is a multidisciplinary approach to facilitating learning and change that has roots in psychology, adult learning, and organizational development.

### Personal Interest in This Topic

My interest in this topic comes from personal experience. As a leadership and business coach I am deeply motivated by the desire to understand processes of human learning and change. When I started my first entrepreneurial coaching group I was already working with several business owners in a dyadic (one-on-one) coaching context. What struck me about this work was that many of my clients reported very similar situations, problem sets, choices, and dilemmas throughout the course of our work together. I began to wonder whether certain experiences in business ownership were inherent in the nature of starting and owning a business, and whether clients would find it valuable to engage collaboratively with their peers in order to learn from common challenges. In 2011, I designed and launched a group coaching program for entrepreneurs in the Boston area and groups have been a part of my practice ever since.

My interest also stems from my belief that group coaching may represent the future of the coaching field. As more individuals and organizations become familiar with the concept of coaching and its benefits, a need is emerging for new and affordable coaching formats. Group coaching provides many of the benefits of dyadic coaching engagements, but at a much lower cost per person. In addition, the group environment offers some benefits that dyadic coaching does not. These aspects of group coaching are discussed in detail in the next chapter.

In my work with groups of entrepreneurs, I noticed group members sharing their personal stories, reflecting on and working through complex problems, and contributing their knowledge and experience to the group. I also witnessed what seemed like group members' identities evolving through learning and exchange, through the acquisition of new resources, and through generative dialogue. I am reminded of Jacqueline (a fictitious name), who struggled with the idea of promoting herself and her business.

## A Case Example From Practice

Jacqueline detested bragging, and believed that promoting herself or her enterprise was obnoxious and wrong. As a result, her business as a Pilates instructor had plateaued. She felt intimidated by the prospect of getting things unstuck, as presumably it would involve bragging and being obnoxious. In our coaching group, we talked about how Jacqueline was making sense of her situation, and about how she might interpret things differently. I pointed out that communication in our culture is gendered—and that girls, in particular, are socialized in such a way that from an early age they learn not to stick out or show off. They learn that bragging is undesirable, and that it leads to negative social consequences (ostracism, bullying, etc.).

This seemed to resonate with other women in the group. Some of them spoke about having experienced similar feelings. They also spoke about how realizing that culture and socialization had likely shaped many of their experiences over the years, was both freeing and frustrating. We talked about whether the way Jacqueline was viewing her situation was something inherited, versus authored. In other words, to what extent was she living out an inherited cultural story, rather than authoring her own? If she were to craft her own story now, how would it differ? I suggested that maybe this wasn't about selling anything. Maybe it was about communicating the value of her work so that people would have the opportunity to benefit from it. What if sharing these opportunities was really an act of generosity and caring? This interpretation seemed to stick, and the group listened, bearing witness, as Jacqueline articulated a new understanding of her situation which revolved around these themes of opportunity, generosity, and caring.

Jacqueline's story serves as an illustration of how learning for entrepreneurs is often stimulated by significant experiences in their lives and supported by various forms of social interaction. EL is thus an experiential *and* a social phenomenon. In the context of the group's conversation, Jacqueline changed her thinking about a specific business situation. As a result, this same situation lacked the "teeth" it had before, and Jacqueline found new power to confront it.

However, at times EL encompasses more than just learning about specific situations. On another level, it can also give shape to an individual's evolving sense of entrepreneurial self-identity or an individual's learning about *who he or she can be* as an entrepreneur. Jacqueline's sense of self also shifted. The notion of her entrepreneurial self as someone "impaired" or "deficient" in some way because of her distaste for self-promotion had given way to a more nuanced understanding. She now understood herself not as impaired, but as *embedded* in a very powerful cultural discourse. The shared experiences of her peers in the group helped legitimize Jacqueline's new understanding of self and situation.

Jacqueline's experience may not be representative of all interactions in entrepreneurial coaching groups. A very high degree of variation exists among group coaching formats, approaches, and methodologies. Yet the potential exists for group-format coaching to actively foster critical reflection and meaning making in entrepreneurs, and to facilitate their coming in from the cold. Jacqueline's story helps illustrate three fundamental learning-related challenges that are discussed in the EL literature and that characterize the learning journeys of many entrepreneurs: *learning how to learn from experience*, *learning with and from other entrepreneurs*, and *constructing and negotiating entrepreneurial identity*. I discuss these challenges in Chapter 2. Together, they helped shape the data-gathering and interpretation phases of this research.

## Overview

In the next chapter I place the study within the literatures on entrepreneurship and group coaching, and discuss theory and research related to common entrepreneurial challenges, entrepreneurial learning, and the role of entrepreneurial identity. Then, I describe several models of group coaching and discuss their respective mechanisms of learning and change. In Chapter 3, I outline the methods of inquiry used in this study, including methods of data collection and interpretation. Chapter 4 contains the study findings. This chapter is organized into three sections representing three different types of phenomena that research participants associated with their meaningful learning experiences in group coaching. In Chapter 5, I discuss the significance of the findings and outline the study's contributions to research and practice.

## CHAPTER TWO: LITERATURE REVIEW

The goal of this study was to explore the experience of group coaching as a setting for entrepreneurial learning and change. Although academic interest in EL has grown in recent years, more research is needed to understand the social processes involved, as well as the different types of social contexts in which EL occurs (Fayolle, Pittaway, Politis, & Toutain, 2014; Wang & Chugh, 2014). Specifically, this study was concerned with individual business owners' experiences of "coming in from the cold," or bringing issues and challenges they might otherwise engage with in isolation into the social context of their coaching groups. A review of the literature did not find any existing studies of the narratives of entrepreneurs who participate in group coaching.

However, I found many narrative accounts in the literatures on entrepreneurship, entrepreneurial learning, and entrepreneurial identity. The literatures on group coaching and related group modalities help illuminate the practical and theoretical basis for coaching in group settings. I organized the following review of the literature around each of these literature areas, and divided it into two main sections.

Relevant literature on the lives and experiences of entrepreneurs begins the review. Included in this section are works that illustrate the challenges inherent in entrepreneurship, the nature of entrepreneurial learning and the mechanisms that support it, and related issues involving the construction and maintenance of entrepreneurial identity. For entrepreneurs, learning is about more than acquiring business knowledge. It is also about the acquisition of identity, or about *learning who one can be* (Higgins & Aspinall, 2011; Rae, 2000). Entrepreneurs face many learning-related challenges, including learning how to engage in critical reflection (Zhang & Hamilton, 2009), "learning to learn" from critical events or crises

(Cope & Watts, 2000; Deakins & Freel, 1998), and acquiring and maintaining a sense of self-as-entrepreneur (Mallett & Wapshott, 2015; Rae, 2000; Watson, 2009). I argue that the distinct challenges of entrepreneurship make learning integral to the entrepreneurial process, and that social interaction plays a key role in entrepreneurial learning.

The second section overviews the literature on group coaching. In this section I define group coaching and discuss various approaches to group coaching practice as well as knowledge from empirical research. I place special emphasis on how the literature conceptualizes the mechanisms of learning and change at work in group coaching settings. Relevant processes include the construction of transitional spaces or holding environments (Kets de Vries, 2014; Thornton, 2010), dialogue and exchange with other group members (Brown & Grant, 2010; Thornton, 2010), and/or collaborative meaning-making (Stelter, Nielsen, & Wikman, 2011). Given what is known about the impact of group and social processes on learning and identity, I argue that more research is needed on how these processes play out in the lives and experiences of entrepreneurs through their participation in group coaching.

## Entrepreneurship

There is an extensive body of literature on entrepreneurship. Within this body, much attention has been paid to stages of organizational growth or "life cycles" of small businesses (Quinn & Cameron, 1983) and to economic perspectives on business development (Watson, 2009). At the individual level of analysis, past research has focused primarily on the psychological aspects of entrepreneurship—for example, the personality traits or characteristics of successful entrepreneurs (Harrison & Leitch, 2005; Watson, 2009).

However, the study of entrepreneurial personalities has been criticized for failing to take into consideration an entrepreneur's ability to learn and change over time and through experience (Gartner, 1988; Rae, 2000; Watson, 2009).

In the wake of this critique, a focus on entrepreneurial learning (EL) has helped reinvigorate the field (Wang & Chugh, 2014) by exploring the learning and developmental processes of entrepreneurship (Deakins & Freel, 1998, 2012) as well as the learning processes that influence "who an entrepreneur becomes" (Rae, 2000). Some assumptions guiding these areas of inquiry are (a) that understanding how and when learning happens is fundamental to understanding the entrepreneurial process (Wang & Chugh, 2014), and (b) that entrepreneurs develop and grow through learning (Cope, 2005).

The section below explores threads from this literature, including *how* and *what* entrepreneurs learn, what kinds of barriers prevent them from learning, and what mechanisms facilitate their learning. Before exploring these questions, it is necessary to consider the nature of the challenges inherent in entrepreneurship—challenges that provide a context for EL, and that make EL fundamentally important to entrepreneurial survival, let alone success.

**Challenges Inherent in Entrepreneurship**

Entrepreneurs engage with a different set of challenges than the organizationally employed—one that requires different avenues for learning and problem solving (Brett, Mullally, O'Gorman, & Fuller-Love, 2012). These challenges reflect the fundamental dynamism of entrepreneurship and the entrepreneurial life, as well as the substantial costs associated with pursuing an entrepreneurial path. I discuss several of these below.

**Fundamentally dynamic.** Entrepreneurship is fundamentally dynamic and non-linear (Cope, 2003; Deakins & Freel, 1998). The turbulence and uncertainty that entrepreneurs face influence the development of their learning practices (Higgins & Aspinall, 2011).  For example, entrepreneurial learning is less likely to occur in a planned or programmatic way, and more likely to occur as a result of knowledge accumulated over time and through reactions to specific situations or experiences (Deakins & Freel, 1998).  "Discontinuous" or non-routine events act as a key mechanism to stimulate higher-order learning that fundamentally alters an individual's assumptions about effective action (Cope, 2003).

*More at stake.*  Entrepreneurs frequently have more at stake in their work than the organizationally employed.  Cope (2003) explained that the relationship between entrepreneurs and their businesses is complex and intimate.  Many entrepreneurs invest significant personal resources in the creation of new ventures.  This, in turn exposes them to "considerable financial, emotional and social risks" (p. 430).  Cope argued that it is precisely these extremes of emotional and financial involvement that make entrepreneurship a unique context in which to study the phenomenon of learning.

*Moving target.*  Entrepreneurs' needs are a moving target—they evolve throughout the business life-cycle (Cope & Watts, 2000).  According to life-cycle theorists, all small businesses face similar growth challenges that advance along a more or less predictable trajectory (Churchill & Lewis, 1983).  In response to these challenges, entrepreneurial firms must develop new management styles and strategies, and entrepreneurs must develop new skills.  For example, as a firm grows and matures, its management is likely to become less centralized, more hierarchical, and more complex.  This requires that owner-managers learn to delegate effectively rather than be personally involved in every decision.

Such a progression demands much individual learning and change on the part of entrepreneurs. However, Cope and Watts (2000) explained that the literature in this area focuses primarily on the growth of the business itself and not on the corresponding developmental trajectory of individual entrepreneurs. In addition, life-cycle growth models in general have been criticized for their rigidity, their deterministic view, and their exclusively internal focus on the crises that drive growth (Deakins & Freel, 2012; McKelvie & Wikland, 2010).

**Substantial costs.** While owning a business can be significantly rewarding, research has found that the rewards often come at a high cost (Alstete, 2008; Boyd & Gumpert, 1983). In a survey of 450 New England entrepreneurs, Boyd and Gumpert (1983) found financial reward, independence, and sense of achievement to be among the biggest benefits of entrepreneurship. Participants reported that being accountable only to themselves, being able to make their own decisions, and being able to implement their own ideas and bring them to fruition, were among the most satisfying rewards. These findings were echoed by Alstete (2008), who interviewed 149 established entrepreneurs in the metropolitan New York area.

When asked about the disadvantages of entrepreneurship, participants mentioned stress, responsibilities and long hours (Alstete, 2008), as well as loneliness and isolation, immersion in business, and people problems (Boyd & Gumpert, 1983). Similar findings were reported by Gumpert and Boyd (1984), Jamal (1997, 2009), and Zhang and Hamilton (2009). The long hours required to achieve success were mentioned as contributing to stress and responsibilities (Alstete, 2008). Participants reported being "on call" all the time, bringing work home, and feeling mentally preoccupied with work when at home. Boyd and Gumpert (1983) found the concerns of professional life to be all-consuming for entrepreneurs—leaving little time for civic engagement, recreational activities, or family and friends. Participants in their study spoke of this as a kind of "personal sacrifice" which entrepreneurship entails.

Jamal (1997, 2009), who studied the differences in the quality of work and non-work life between the self- and organizationally employed, found that self-employed individuals experienced higher job stress, burnout, and health problems than the organizationally employed. In addition, and contrary to prevailing logic, the self-employed *did not* experience higher levels of job satisfaction than the organizationally employed, but this outcome may depend on the self-selectivity of entrepreneurial career paths. It is presumed that those who are forced into entrepreneurial careers as a result of a layoff or other loss of employment may not find entrepreneurship to be as satisfying as those who self-select.

*Isolation and loneliness*. Chief among the costs or disadvantages of entrepreneurship is the experience of feeling isolated and alone (Boyd & Gumpert, 1983; Gumpert & Boyd, 1984; Zhang & Hamilton, 2009). According to Boyd and Gumpert (1983), although entrepreneurs are usually surrounded by others (employees, vendors, customers, competitors, etc.), "they are isolated from persons in whom they can confide" (p. 46). There are several reasons why.

First, the demands of work (especially the long hours) may prevent entrepreneurs from reaching out to friends and family for support (Boyd & Gumpert, 1983). However, entrepreneurs may also withdraw from friends and family simply because family members don't or can't understand, or because they have conflicting values related to work-life balance (Gumpert & Boyd, 1984). Zhang and Hamilton (2009) found that entrepreneurs are reluctant to confide in friends and family even when they do have time. An interview excerpt from Rose, a participant in their study, explains why:

Unless they're in business, their perspective is slightly skewed I think, because for

example my ex-boyfriend, his view was always "well, you're the boss, you just do

what you want", and in theory as the boss you can just do what you want, but in

practice you need to take your team with you. You can't just impose from above. And

because he'd always been an employee and always experienced business where

things always were imposed from above, and he felt not included in the loop. That

was his view. And I think while friends and family can be invaluable, unless they

have some experience of running a business, the advice tends to be not objective.

What they want to do is help you feel better. (p. 615)

In essence, friends and family tend not to be objective, and unless they're involved in

running a business of their own, they often lack the knowledge and experience to be of help.

Zhang and Hamilton (2009) found that the isolation participants experienced was not

simply about finding someone else to talk to about business.  It was about finding someone to

talk to *about problems*.  In Gumpert and Boyd's (1984) study, 68% of survey respondents

reported not having a confidant with whom they could "share their deep concerns" (p. 19).

In both studies, this finding came across as a reluctance to show weakness or to admit

ignorance or difficulty.  Participants spoke of a perceived need to project an image of

strength, health, and reliability to suppliers and customers (Zhang & Hamilton, 2009), to hide

weakness from competitors, and to convey confidence to employees (Gumpert & Boyd,

1984).  As a result, entrepreneurs often lack colleagues or peers with whom they feel

comfortable sharing ideas, processing experiences, or even simply commiserating.

In addition, events that bill themselves as peer networking opportunities often fail to

establish a sufficient level of trust and openness to foster meaningful communication.  Events and conferences organized by professional associations or governmental agencies, for example, are more likely to be regarded by entrepreneurs as sales opportunities, which further encourage the projection of a professional image (Zhang & Hamilton, 2009). In addition, these events are often short-term and fleeting, which prevents people from getting to know one another well enough to speak openly about their problems. This contributes to a sense of isolation.

In a larger sense however, these findings raise important questions about the appropriateness and conduciveness of different relationships to sharing business problems. While the reluctance to show weakness is portrayed as an internal or subjective (self-imposed) pressure (Gumpert & Boyd, 1984), the context in which communication is considered also makes a difference. Research has shown that participation in peer learning programs with other non-competitive business owners fosters open communication, along with critical reflection and learning (Florén, 2003; Zhang & Hamilton, 2009). In a peer learning context, people develop trust and open up in ways that allow them to admit a lack of knowledge and/or to talk about problems that everyone has, but no one will publicly admit to. From this point of view, a reluctance to confide or show weakness may simply reflect a degree of pragmatism, and the absence of a dedicated peer learning network.

In any case, research shows that for entrepreneurs, isolation and loneliness go hand in hand (Boyd & Gumpert, 1983). The independence and freedom that characterize entrepreneurial positions may actually serve to keep loneliness concealed. Entrepreneurs clearly value their freedom, and as a result, they tend to lean toward solitary activities (Gumpert & Boyd, 1984). According to Boyd and Gumpert (1983), all of these factors—a lack of anyone to confide in, withdrawal from family and friends, a reluctance to show weakness or admit difficulty, and an inclination toward solitary activity—contribute to the experience of loneliness.

**Summary.** As shown above, entrepreneurs face a different set of challenges than the organizationally employed. The dynamic nature of entrepreneurship means that many entrepreneurs face high levels of turbulence and uncertainty, while taking great financial, emotional, and social risks in order to pursue their entrepreneurial paths. In addition, as small businesses grow, their management challenges evolve, placing additional learning demands on their owner-managers. The literature shows that the demands of entrepreneurship overwhelmingly dominate the lives of entrepreneurs (Alstete, 2008; Boyd & Gumpert, 1983; Jamal, 1997, 2009). Despite being surrounded by other people for much of the time, entrepreneurs experience significant isolation and loneliness (Boyd & Gumpert, 1983; Gumpert & Boyd, 1984; Zhang & Hamilton, 2009).

Scholars suggest that peer learning networks can play a role in alleviating the experience of isolation and loneliness. The next section discusses the benefits of effective peer learning in the context of EL, as well as the conditions necessary for creating effective peer learning environments. To establish a foundation, the section first explores what is known about EL in general, including *how* and *what* entrepreneurs learn, what kinds of barriers prevent them from learning, and what kinds of mechanisms facilitate their learning.

## Entrepreneurial Learning

Wang and Chugh's (2014) systematic review of the literature found 11 explicit and 10 implicit definitions of EL across 47 articles using the term, "entrepreneurial learning." These definitions vary according to a range of theoretical perspectives (i.e., learning theories), learning types, and contexts. However, nearly all are fundamentally aligned in their concern with *what* and *how* individual entrepreneurs learn. This study focused on what and how individual entrepreneurs learn *from their group coaching experiences*. Therefore, experiential (D. A. Kolb, 1984), organizational (Argyris & Schön, 1978; Burgoyne & Hodgson, 1983), and social/contextual (Lave & Wenger, 1991; Wenger, 1999) theories of learning were important to consider in adopting a working definition of EL for the study.

I began with Rae's (2006) social/experiential definition of EL: "learning to recognise and act on [entrepreneurial] opportunities, through initiating, organising and managing ventures in social and behavioural ways" (p. 40). In keeping with the constructivist orientation of the study, however, I found it important to acknowledge the processes through which participants *construct* new meaning in relation to their experiences. I therefore incorporated Rae and Carswell's (2001) focus on the construction of meaning into my working definition. For the purpose of this study, EL is defined as *the construction of new meaning in the process of recognizing and acting on opportunities, through initiating, organizing, and managing ventures in social and behavioral ways.*

Research on EL has emerged partly in response to a past preoccupation with the psychology of entrepreneurship, which involves the study of personality traits and characteristics of entrepreneurs (Harrison & Leitch, 2005; Watson, 2009). This philosophical position assumes the character of the entrepreneur to be relatively stable and unchanging, and therefore amenable to categorization (Jones & Spicer, 2005). However, research in this tradition has failed to capture evidence of a set of universal, defining characteristics of the entrepreneur (Baum & Locke, 2004), and the notion of entrepreneurial character has been criticized for failing to take into consideration an entrepreneur's ability to learn and change

(Gartner, 1988; Rae, 2000; Watson, 2009).

In response, EL research has focused on studying the ways that learning and development shape entrepreneurial activities and the changing identities of entrepreneurs (Deakins & Freel, 1998, 2012; Rae, 2000). In the section below I discuss several contributions from the relevant literatures on experiential, organizational, and social/contextual learning in an entrepreneurial context. Drawing on Wang and Chugh's (2014) framing of the EL literature, I also highlight some of the issues and debates relevant to each of these areas.

**Experiential Learning Perspectives**

The literature shows that EL is primarily experience-based (Higgins & Aspinall, 2011; Zhang & Hamilton, 2009), and learning from experience is understood to be a key ability in entrepreneurship (Deakins & Freel, 1998). Entrepreneurial knowledge is most often gained through action taken in response to lived experiences and real world situations, rather than through formal instruction (Higgins & Aspinall, 2011). While some degree of formal training may be helpful, it cannot substitute for learning that comes from actual participation in entrepreneurial activity (Deakins & Freel, 1998). In essence, entrepreneurs learn by doing, and by reacting to specific issues and experiences.

Researchers have focused on two related concepts which are central to experiential learning in an entrepreneurial context. The first is the idea that entrepreneurship is characterized by critical learning events (Deakins & Freel, 1998). The second involves the role that critical reflection plays in learning (Cope, 2003; Cope & Watts, 2000; Zhang & Hamilton, 2009). I discuss each of these below, and then explore common constraints that can limit reflection and experiential learning for entrepreneurs. I then discuss the limitations of the research in this area before concluding with a short summary.

**Critical learning events**. The idea that critical episodes and events can act as catalysts for learning has roots in Mezirow's (1991) theory of transformative learning. In Mezirow's view, these critical episodes could be described as *disorienting dilemmas*, or situations that pose a fundamental challenge to an individual's habitual ways of knowing. Mezirow (2003) theorized that these kinds of challenges stimulate critical reflection and learning that transforms problematic frames of reference (habits of mind, mindsets, meaning perspectives, etc.) to make them "more inclusive, discriminating, open... [and] reflective" (p. 58).

According to Deakins and Freel (1998), entrepreneurship is characterized by "significant and critical learning events" (p. 153). In their multi-case study, participants recounted critical experiences breaking into a close-knit industry, starting a new venture from scratch, navigating a major financial crisis, purchasing a second firm, and persevering through the retirement and succession of a founding team member. These experiences were observed and tracked over the course of 5-6 semi-structured interviews in order to understand the processes that led to each event, how the event was resolved, and what was learned from it.

Deakins and Freel (1998) found that all of these experiences served as catalysts for learning specific entrepreneurial abilities or competencies—for example, the ability to network, to assimilate experience and opportunity, to learn from past strategies and mistakes, to access resources, and to assemble an effective entrepreneurial team (pp. 150-153). Their study also demonstrated that in these cases, critical learning and growth opportunities occurred unpredictably, and without adequate training or preparation for the entrepreneurs.

As a result, learning and ability advanced through discontinuous "jumps" (p. 152) in response to specific problems unfolding in real time. Deakins and Freel claimed that the success of a firm depends on the ability of the entrepreneur to "maximize knowledge as a result of experiencing these learning events" (p. 153).

However, viewing critical incidents as discrete and isolated phenomena may not sufficiently capture their complexity or significance. In a phenomenological case study of six entrepreneurs, Cope and Watts (2000) found that entrepreneurs often face prolonged and traumatic critical "periods" or episodes, rather than discrete events with clear temporal and perceptual boundaries. While emotionally charged and difficult to resolve, these episodes were viewed by participants as significantly influential in terms of their learning and self-awareness.

More importantly, it was evident from participants' storied accounts that these critical episodes do not occur independently of any entrepreneur. Instead, they involve "a change in perception and awareness that stimulates the entrepreneur into action" (Cope & Watts, 2000, p. 113). In one example, an entrepreneur recalled making a serious marketing mistake that led to a financial crisis for his enterprise, and subsequently to a series of actions taken to resolve the situation. The entire critical episode involved many discrete events over time, inextricably linked and bound by context.

This finding echoes Deakins and Freel (1998), who asserted that learning occurs when reactions to critical events require the entrepreneur to process information in new ways, to adapt strategy, and to make important decisions. In many ways, learning and action are intertwined. EL involves change and difference that are enacted through language and behavior, not only through cognition (Rae, 2000). What the entrepreneur actually does must change in order for it to be considered learning. In other words, entrepreneurs must identify the opportunities that arise out of experience and act on them (Deakins & Freel, 1998). The key to translating critical events or crises into actionable learning opportunities lies in critical reflection (Argyris & Schön, 1978; Mezirow, 1991), which I discuss next.

**Critical reflection.** D. A. Kolb (1984) referred to *reflective observation* as the mechanism responsible for transforming concrete experience into abstract concepts. In the context of entrepreneurial activity, critical learning events are defined by their ability to stimulate deep reflection that leads to experiential learning (Cope, 2003, 2005). The literature portrays this type of deep reflection as integral to effective EL (Cope & Watts, 2000; Zhang & Hamilton, 2009). In particular, critical reflection plays a key role in determining the learning and developmental outcomes of critical events in entrepreneurs' lives. One participant in Cope and Watts' (2000) study, for example, described experiencing his most significant learning through the process of retroactively reflecting on the actions he had taken during a crisis.

Reflectivity is described as "critical" when it generates insight into the underlying values and perceptions that shape behavior, leading to changes in self-awareness and personal understanding (Cope & Watts, 2000; Zhang & Hamilton, 2009). On a practical level, this kind of reflection involves "activity in which people recapture their experience, think about it, and mull it over, and evaluate it" (p. 49). While critical reflection is often thought of as a retrospective activity, it can also be proactive (Cope, 2005; Cope & Watts, 2000). Proactive reflection involves the "bringing forward" of experience (Gibb, 1997), or the extrapolation of one's learning from past critical events in order to anticipate or predict potential future events before they happen (Cope, 2005; Cope & Watts, 2000).

Whether retrospective or proactive, the processes described above involve reflecting *on* past or future actions and experiences. However, it is also possible to reflect *in the midst of* action, as Schön's (1983) seminal work on reflective practice illustrates. Schön theorized that professionals in practice draw from tacit knowledge when performing repetitive or routinized work. But when surprised by new or unique situations, they must grapple to make sense of these phenomena while they are still unfolding. In other words, they must think on their feet as they reflect *in* action.

Reflection-in-action (Schön, 1983) involves turning thought "back on action and on the knowing which is implicit in action" (p. 50). It is through this process that an individual may surface and criticize his or her implicit grasp of a situation, to construct a new understanding, and to test that new understanding through experimentation. This process is not always instantaneous, but is bounded by context. Reflection-in-action is "bounded by the 'action-present'" (p. 62), the time period during which the situation can still be influenced by action. Such time can stretch over minutes or months, depending on the characteristics of the situation at hand.

These perspectives illustrate the importance of critical reflection to the experiential learning process. Indeed, learning from experience or crisis *requires* critical reflection (Cope & Watts, 2000; Zhang & Hamilton, 2009). Unfortunately, the nature of entrepreneurship presents certain constraints which frequently limit critical reflection and constrain learning for entrepreneurs.

**Constraints on experiential learning.** A number of constraints that are inherently characteristic of entrepreneurship act as barriers to reflection and learning (Brett et al., 2012; Higgins & Aspinall, 2011; Zhang & Hamilton, 2009). The principal issue here is one of resources, including but not limited to time, knowledge, and experience. First and foremost, constraints on time often prevent entrepreneurs from engaging in reflective thinking (Brett et al., 2012; Zhang & Hamilton, 2009). Time is typically viewed by entrepreneurs as extremely limited, and some may feel as though their time is too valuable to be spent reflecting (Zhang & Hamilton, 2009). Time constraints may be physical (e.g., due to limited human resources), or they may stem from the prioritization of day-to-day work, or of "doing" over thinking. Whether the constraints are physical or subjective, entrepreneurs face a potential trade-off in terms of time when they choose to engage in critical reflection.

Second, isolation (discussed above) can function as a barrier to learning (Brett et al., 2012). Operating in isolation, entrepreneurs may bare sole concern for policy-related or strategic issues, and may lack appropriate others with whom to reflectively discuss problems (Gumpert & Boyd, 1984; Zhang & Hamilton, 2009). As a result, this lack of input from others (especially peers) can hamper learning and negatively affect decision making, while increasing the pressure associated with making important decisions (Gumpert & Boyd, 1984). As discussed below, social processes are an important factor in EL, and a lack of social interaction makes learning less likely to occur.

Third, a lack of knowledge and experience can prevent critical reflection and learning (Brett et al., 2012; Higgins & Aspinall, 2011). Entrepreneurs may not always know *how* to reflect or *what* to reflect on (Zhang & Hamilton, 2009), and/or they may lack the experience or skills to engage in critical reflection (Higgins & Aspinall, 2011). Boyd and Gumpert (1983), for example, wrote that the entrepreneurs they interviewed were not inclined toward introspection. Several indicated that their participation in the interview itself was the longest period they had spent reflecting on things—yet all found it to be time well spent. In light of these facts, Higgins and Aspinall (2011) proposed that entrepreneurs often need some kind of conceptual framework to help organize their reflection and to facilitate learning. An effective conceptual framework could take the shape of an organized peer learning group or mentoring program, for example, that prioritizes critical reflection.

**Limitations and questions.** Although much of the EL literature is grounded in an experiential learning perspective, more research is needed on how experiential learning processes occur in entrepreneurial contexts. Wang and Chugh (2014), for example, called for new research that can contribute to an understanding of how the entire experiential learning cycle (from concrete experience through reflective observation, to abstract conceptualization, to experimentation which produces new concrete experiences, etc.) unfolds for entrepreneurs or in entrepreneurial firms. In addition, much of what has been written has focused exclusively on individual cognition while largely ignoring the social processes and contexts that contribute to an individual's learning (Fayolle et al., 2014; Wang & Chugh, 2014). To address these issues, Wang and Chugh (2014) recommended that researchers explore related questions, such as, "What factors play a key role in each stage of the experiential learning cycle?" and "What and how do entrepreneurs or entrepreneurial firms learn from the experience (successes and failures) of other entrepreneurs or entrepreneurial firms?" (p. 39).

**Summary.** Learning from experience is a key aspect of EL and a fundamentally important ability in entrepreneurship. Critical learning events can provide a catalyst for learning specific entrepreneurial competencies, as well as for learning that leads to new awareness or new perspectives. Critical reflection is a key mechanism and driving force for transforming these experiences into learning and developmental outcomes, but entrepreneurs often face constraints on their time and other resources that limit critical reflection. Critiques of the EL literature have resulted in calls for more research that explores the entire experiential learning cycle in entrepreneurial contexts, and that takes into account the social processes and contexts which contribute to EL. Researchers agree that EL is fundamentally experiential in nature. However, learning can occur on multiple levels, and acquired knowledge can take many forms. In the next section I explore organizational learning perspectives rooted in Bateson's (1972) theory of learning types, including theories advanced by Argyris and Schön (1978) and Burgoyne and Hodgson (1983). Despite their organizational focus, these theories also shed light on the varied and multileveled learning processes which unfold in individuals.

**Organizational Learning Perspectives**

Knowledge derived from entrepreneurial experience can reflect different levels of learning (Cope & Watts, 2000; Higgins & Aspinall, 2011). Organizational learning theory tends to be concerned with how *whole* organizations (as opposed to individuals) learn. However, organizational learning theorists such as Argyris and Schön (1978) and Burgoyne and Hodgson (1983) have contributed significantly to an understanding of how individuals learn in organizational settings. Their perspectives are rooted in Bateson's (1972) seminal work on the logical categories of learning and communication.

Bateson (1972) described how learning in individuals can occur on different "ordered" levels. What Bateson (1972) called *Learning I* is characterized by a revision of choice within a set of alternatives. Learning I occurs when feedback compels someone to select a different option, make a different choice, or take a different action from among a set of options, choices, or actions. In contrast, *Learning II* refers to "a corrective change in the set of alternatives from which choice is made" (p. 293). In other words, Learning II occurs when an individual steps back to examine the set itself and identifies new options, choices, or actions for altering the set. *Learning III* represents a change to the system of sets of options from which choice is made.

**Multi-leveled learning models.** Argyris and Schön (1978) and Burgoyne and Hodgson (1983) later adapted Bateson's ideas about learning in individuals for application in organizational and managerial contexts. Argyris and Schön (1978) proposed a framework to distinguish between two fundamentally different levels of learning—"single-loop" learning, and "double-loop" learning. Single-loop learning (encompassing Learning 1 and 2 above) is most often described as adaptive in nature. It is characterized by changes to existing actions or strategies in light of feedback generated through observation of the consequences of past actions. While learning at this level leads to new practices, the underlying "theories of action" that shape these practices remain unchanged.

Double-loop learning, in contrast, requires that learners critically examine their underlying theories of action, or the values and assumptions that guide their notions of effective action (Argyris & Schön, 1978; Cope, 2003). Cope (2003), for example, described how a participant named Andrew experienced double-loop learning as a result of a critical event involving a conflict with an employee. Though painful and difficult, the conflict caused Andrew to examine his own assumptions about how his employees should behave, and about his own role in managing the company. This led to significant change and the formalization of new systems to prevent the same problems from recurring.

Cope and Watts (2000) explained how a critical episode triggered a shift in self-awareness for one participant, which "fundamentally changed his outlook on how he conducted his business and his life" (p. 114). Such events or episodes are indicative of "higher-level learning"—learning that can reframe an individual's understanding of the past, and help him or her prevent future incidents from occurring (Cope & Watts, 2000). Higher-level learning, in effect, involves "learning how to learn" from experience.

According to Higgins and Aspinall (2011), many entrepreneurs become proficient at single-loop, adaptive learning—responding to changes in the environment, correcting problems, adopting new methods, and so on. However, learning in these situations rarely involves critical reflection. Thus, the underlying values of the firm, and/or the entrepreneur's theories of action, remain unexamined and unchanged. Small firms cannot prosper from adaptive learning alone. In order to survive and grow, entrepreneurs must reflect critically on their own thoughts, feelings, and underlying assumptions.

Burgoyne and Hodgson (1983) adopted a similar framework for learning that takes place on three different levels. "Level 1 learning" occurs when an individual simply acquires new information which has an immediate impact on a situation at hand, without any long-term effect. An example of this could be a manager learning that a particular product is no longer being produced in-house, and is instead being ordered from an outside source. The information is factual and relevant, but has no impact on the manager's worldview in general.

Learning that takes place on "Level 2" reflects the acquisition of new knowledge that exhibits transferability beyond the present situation, yet is still specific to a particular type of situation, from the manager's point of view (Burgoyne & Hodgson, 1983). For example, a manager being caught off guard by an unexpected situation could cause her or him to be more alert in the future to similar situations arising, and may lead to new ways of coping with or avoiding said situations. A manager may even adopt "case laws" which establish precedents for responding to similar situations.

In a cumulative fashion, knowledge of such cases over time can gradually shift the manager's tacit attitudes or orientations toward things, events, or people.  Burgoyne and Hodgson (1983) described this as a gradual change in "background consciousness," such as when a manager slowly changes his or her opinion about a customer or employee over the course of many interactions, without being consciously aware of the change.  They explained that Level 2 learning can also occur through deliberate problem-solving, or through reflective learning.  In deliberate problem-solving, a manager may proactively search for a solution to a problem through exploration and experimentation.  An example might involve realizing that one's current time management system is not working, and consequently learning about and trying out different systems.  Reflective learning occurs when managers are able to think about a particular problem and reflect on it while they are not directly engaged with it.  Reflective moments can lead to critical insights and new ideas.

Finally, "Level 3 learning" (Burgoyne & Hodgson, 1983) occurs when a manager becomes conscious about "his conceptions of the world in general, how they were formed, or how he might change them" (p. 395).  In their study, Burgoyne and Hodgson recounted the story of one manager who, through an incident with an employee, became aware of her tendency to expect too much from other people, and subsequently attempted to change her approach.  Another manager spoke of becoming conscious of her tendency to get irritated in certain situations, and of how she ought to work on controlling that.  Burgoyne and Hodgson remarked that incidents reflecting Level 3 learning were comparatively rare in their study.  Lower-level learning was far more prevalent.

**Challenges and questions.**  Wang and Chugh (2014) noted that lower-level and higher-level learning correspond to the entrepreneurial processes of opportunity exploration and opportunity exploitation:

> Adaptive and lower-level learning involves modifying actions according to the
> difference between expected and obtained outcomes (hence exploitative in nature),
> whereas generative and higher-level learning involves questioning the values,
> assumptions and policies that lead to the actions in the first place, and searching and
> discovering new solutions (hence exploratory in nature). (p. 38)

While both of these processes are necessary in entrepreneurship (Shane & Venkataraman, 2000), more research is needed to understand how entrepreneurs learn to develop the different sets of skills and resources required for both exploration and exploitation. To address this issue, Wang and Chugh (2014) suggested that researchers explore related questions, such as, "How does the learning of entrepreneurs or entrepreneurial firms differ in the processes of exploration and exploitation?" and "What cognitive processes do entrepreneurs go through in different learning contexts?" (p. 38).

In addition, Zahra, Abdelgawad, and Tsang (2011) discussed the importance of "unlearning" (the intentional discarding of practices) in setting the stage for or inducing the actions or activities that can lead to learning. Wang and Chugh (2014) argued that higher-level (exploratory) learning involves a high degree of unlearning (e.g., distinguishing from failure what is not working and changing it). A key question for future research in this vein is, what and how do entrepreneurs actually unlearn?

**Summary.** Learning from experience can occur on multiple levels, and acquired knowledge can take many forms. Learning can be described as either lower-level, which consists of adaptive changes to existing strategies for dealing with specific situations or types of situations; or higher-level, which involves changes to underlying values or orientations toward self and world in general. Further research is needed in this area to understand how entrepreneurs engage in both lower-level (exploitative) and higher-level (exploratory) learning, as well as what and how entrepreneurs unlearn when they engage in higher-level learning. The section that follows discusses the nature of social interaction in EL, the requisites for effective social learning environments, and the benefits available to entrepreneurs who engage in them.

**Social/Contextual Learning Perspectives**

As Jarvis (2012) wrote, "Learning is not just a psychological process that happens in splendid isolation from the world in which the learner lives" (p. 11). All learning occurs within a social context. A social learning perspective holds that learning is the product of social interaction or participation in the social practices of the communities to which one belongs (Lave & Wenger, 1991; Wenger, 2009). Learning is therefore a collective process and a situated activity, shaped as much by sociocultural influences as by the specific situation at hand.

Higgins and Aspinall (2011) argued that learning in small firms is based on contextualized action and social interaction. EL is highly contextual. Entrepreneurial issues and experiences do not occur in a vacuum. They are situated within an entrepreneur's environment and social interactions, and enacted through practice (Higgins, Mirza, & Drozynska, 2013), which is "emergent, negotiated, and temporary in character" (p. 472). As practice changes, so does knowing. Entrepreneurs must learn by reacting to specific incidents and problems they encounter in practice, as well as from the decisions and mistakes that they make, from their interactions with customers and competitors, and from failure (Deakins & Freel, 1998).

Although research suggests that entrepreneurs often feel isolated and alone, it is also true that social processes play a key role in EL (Cope, 2005; Hamilton, 2006; Higgins & Aspinall, 2011).  Cope and Watts (2000) explained that entrepreneurs frequently need help or support translating the critical events they experience into opportunities for higher-level learning.  This example highlights the importance of social processes in supporting EL, as well as the need for social contexts which can help facilitate learning.  Discussion of two social contexts key to learning for entrepreneurs follows: mentorship and peer learning.

**Mentorship.**  Social interaction in the form of mentorship can aid entrepreneurs in re-conceptualizing critical events as learning events.  Cope and Watts wrote that in order to fulfill this role, mentorship programs should aim to stimulate "proactive reflection on what happened and how effectively the problem or opportunity was dealt with" (p. 118).

The role of the mentor in this context is twofold (Cope & Watts, 2000): first, "to simply 'be there' for the entrepreneur when they are actually going through a critical incident" (p. 117), and to encourage them to step back and engage in reflection.  Second, to help the entrepreneur "bring forward" past experiences in order to examine them critically.  The point of this examination is to help the entrepreneur understand what happened, how it contributed to where the company stands now, and how to apply that learning proactively by anticipating and responding effectively to similar experiences in the future.

**Peer learning.**  Personal (peer) networks are an important learning domain for entrepreneurs (Brett et al., 2012; Zhang & Hamilton, 2009).  Comparatively less research has been done on the benefits of peer advice than on the benefits of professional advice in an entrepreneurial context (Kuhn, Galloway, & Collins-Williams, 2016).  However, the role of peer interaction in EL is much more relevant to this study, given that many organized peer learning networks or programs have much in common with group coaching.

The term "peer learning" as it is used here encompasses many types of organized peer interaction in which individual (versus collective) EL is the focus. Examples include owner-manager peer groups (Zhang & Hamilton, 2009), synergistic learning groups (Collins, Smith, & Hannon, 2006), peer advisory groups (Kuhn et al., 2016), collaborative learning groups (Florén, 2003), and entrepreneurial learning networks (Brett et al., 2012). While subtle differences in design, theoretical orientation, and practice exist between these different examples, they share much in common. More to the point is what these approaches convey about peer learning environments taken as a whole—particularly related to the beneficial impact of peer learning for entrepreneurs, and to the requisite conditions that allow for peer learning to take place in an entrepreneurial context.

*Beneficial impact.* Entrepreneurial peer groups or networks can provide a fertile context for learning by removing barriers or constraints on EL (Brett et al., 2012). In particular, peer networks can help ease isolation and loneliness, spread useful knowledge and ideas, and foster critical reflection and vicarious learning (Florén, 2003; Gumpert & Boyd, 1984; Zhang & Hamilton, 2009). The learning that takes place through peer interaction can be adaptive, or may involve higher-level processes, or a combination of both.

*Reducing isolation and loneliness.* As discussed above, isolation for entrepreneurs is often a result of not having anyone in whom to confide, or with whom to share and commiserate about the pressures of owning a business. Peer support helps reduce isolation by virtue of the fact that peers inherently share the same problems and can personally relate to each other's challenges (Kuhn et al., 2016; Zhang & Hamilton, 2009). Peers recognize and share common problems, despite differences in industry or business type, by virtue of their "peer-ness." Learning in peer networks can overcome feelings of isolation and foster

self-confidence, but not because peers necessarily share the same answers to common

challenges. Rather, these beneficial effects stem from the fact that entrepreneurs *share the

same types of problems* (Zhang & Hamilton, 2009).

In addition, common feelings of isolation and loneliness may actually "precondition"

entrepreneurs to participate in and benefit from peer learning opportunities when they arise.

According to Zhang and Hamilton (2009), the lack of learning opportunities in their other

personal networks (family, customers, employees, vendors, competitors, etc.) results in the

recognition that new learning opportunities are needed. In turn, this recognition can manifest

as a readiness to engage with and learn from peers. In the context of this study, this notion

raises the question of whether and how the specific challenges and learning needs of

entrepreneurs may motivate them to seek out and benefit from group coaching or other

similar peer learning environments.

*Knowledge and ideas.* Individual peers may possess relevant knowledge or

experience, in which case networking with them can provide access to specialized and timely

knowledge (Brett et al., 2012; Kuhn & Galloway, 2015). Over time, networking and

collaboration between firms can establish a pool of best practices derived from collective

knowledge (Brett et al., 2012). When conducted with an EL focus, peer interaction can also

help stimulate the creation and exchange of new ideas, facilitate knowledge sharing through

new connections, and provide useful opportunities for personal development (Brett et al.,

2012; Collins et al., 2006; Gumpert & Boyd, 1984).

*Critical reflection.* While peer learning may aid entrepreneurs in solving concrete

business problems or acquiring specific skills, it can also support the organization of new ideas and/or the resolution of complex decisions (Collins et al., 2006). In this case, the role of peers is not necessarily to solve an individual's problems for them, but rather to help them clarify their thinking and consider alternative points of view (Zhang & Hamilton, 2009). This kind of clarification can represent a challenge to an individual's existing values and perceptions, which in turn can stimulate critical reflection and higher-level learning.

Critical reflection is considered a key mechanism through which EL occurs in peer networks (Florén, 2003; Zhang & Hamilton, 2009). According to Zhang and Hamilton (2009), exposure to alternative points of view helps entrepreneurs become more open and reflect critically on their own practices. Peer learning environments can proactively trigger reflection by encouraging the questioning of individuals' behaviors and assumptions (Florén, 2003). Of particular interest to Zhang and Hamilton (2009) was the fact that questioning and disagreement from peers seem to have a stronger impact on learning than consensus.

*Vicarious learning.* Finally, Zhang and Hamilton (2009) claimed that opportunities to observe or reflect on others' experiences contribute to the value of peer learning. Although learning from critical events is often portrayed as an internal cognitive phenomenon, reflection and learning can also be triggered by external events (i.e., the experiences of peers). In theory, this suggests that peer learning may lower the costs associated with experiential learning by allowing peers to learn from the mistakes and failures of others, without experiencing those failures directly.

***Requisite conditions.*** The research on entrepreneurial peer learning (EPL) refers to several conditions, which when present contribute to making peer learning environments effective. They include a sufficient level of trust, a long-term commitment, and personal accountability.

*Trust.* Establishing a sufficient level of trust allows members of a group to let their guard down (Florén, 2003). This means there is less pressure to maintain "a professional front" or image (p. 215), making it more comfortable for members to pose questions or admit a lack of knowledge. Trust is fundamentally important to peer learning (Zhang & Hamilton, 2009), and the lack of trust present at many networking events, conferences, and professional seminars is one reason why they tend to be ineffective at supporting EL.

Trust and psychological safety are key to encouraging a fertile exchange of ideas and the sharing of personal experiences (Collins et al., 2006). Openness follows trust. An openness between entrepreneurs allows for the discussion of problems and challenges that everyone experiences, but no one can admit to in public (Zhang & Hamilton, 2009). This supports the notion that EPL may lower the costs associated with entrepreneurship, by providing opportunities to reflect on and solve costly problems that would normally be too risky to acknowledge outside of a trusted group of peers.

*Commitment.* Long-term commitment, another prerequisite for EPL, allows trust to develop between members, and to increase over time (Florén, 2003). Experiences shared between individuals over time help peers become familiar with each other's enterprises and problems or challenges. This allows for deeper and richer discussions to unfold in ways that aren't possible in shorter-term approaches to learning.

Zhang and Hamilton (2009) echoed this finding, and explained that long-term, stable peer networks provide time for members to get to know one another and to overcome their competitive mentalities. Strong relations with a small group of peers leads to sharing of both personal and business information. Without a long-term commitment to participating in this type of dialogue, a sufficient level of trust and safety cannot be developed. This in turn greatly constrains possibilities for EL.

Cope and Watts (2000) advised that support for EL must be long-term, contextual, and individualized in order to be effective. In peer learning environments where trust has been established and members have formed lasting relationships, learning is contextualized through the sharing of personal experiences. However, as stated above, learning and action are intimately connected in EL. Sharing and reflecting on shared experience aren't necessarily enough to sustain a peer learning group or network. Action is also critically important (Brett et al., 2012).

*Accountability.* Brett et al. (2012) argued that in terms of building sustainable peer learning networks, a focus on personal accountability helps ensure that members actually implement change. In effective EPL, individuals become accountable to each other for implementing the ideas and changes that result from group discussion. Brett et al. recommended that EPL programs adopt an ethos of accountability, where members report the result of changes they implement in-between meetings. Such an ethos suggests that members need also discuss instances when individuals fail to take actions they committed to.

**Debates and questions.** A well-known debate in the entrepreneurship literature centers on whether entrepreneurial opportunities are discovered or created (Buenstorf, 2007). The main issue is whether opportunities exist independently of the entrepreneur (awaiting discovery) or whether they are created by leaps of perception or interpretation on the part of entrepreneurs. A social/contextual learning perspective enriches this debate and introduces possibilities for future research.

As noted by Wang and Chugh (2014), the two positions of opportunity discovery and opportunity creation correspond to two distinct learning types: *sensing* and *intuitive*. These were originally developed as personality types by Jung (1971). Sensing learning relies on information received externally through the senses, while intuitive learning relies on internal conceptualization (Wang & Chugh, 2014). In entrepreneurship, sensing learning corresponds to the identification or discovery of existing opportunities in the external market environment, whereas intuitive learning corresponds to the creation of new opportunities based on abstract or creative conceptualization.

The research on EPL shows that the social processes involved in peer learning can facilitate both learning types; that is, learning that is external or concrete (acquiring new business knowledge and ideas from others), and learning that is internal or abstract (learning about one's own values and perceptions). However, more research is needed to understand the roles of intuitive and sensing learning, and how social processes can either support or inhibit them. A key question resulting from this discussion is how entrepreneurs search for and acquire external information, and how they make sense of this information through the learning process (Wang & Chugh, 2014). In addition, although previous research on mentorship and EPL has focused on the outcomes associated with participating in such contexts, more research is needed to explore other social contexts in which EL occurs, and to understand the social processes that support and inhibit sensing and intuitive learning in those other contexts.

**Summary.** Although entrepreneurs can often find themselves feeling isolated and alone, social processes play a key role in EL (Cope, 2005; Hamilton, 2006; Higgins & Aspinall, 2011). Social interaction can help entrepreneurs learn from past events by encouraging critical reflection and supporting action and decision making (Florén, 2003; Zhang & Hamilton, 2009). Peer learning networks or programs can help ease isolation (a fundamental barrier to EL) by virtue of the fact that peers share common problems and

personally relate to each other's challenges.  In addition to the therapeutic benefit of

"universality" itself (Yalom & Leszcz, 2005), overcoming isolation can help entrepreneurs

gain access to timely knowledge, develop best practices and new skills, create and exchange

new ideas, and clarify their thinking (Brett et al., 2012; Collins et al., 2006; Kuhn &

Galloway, 2015).

EPL can also help challenge entrepreneurs' existing values and perceptions, and help

encourage the questioning of long-held behaviors and assumptions.  This stimulates critical

reflection that leads to higher-level learning (Florén, 2003; Zhang & Hamilton, 2009).  In

order for EPL to be effective, a sufficient level of trust and safety must be established.  The

long-term commitment of participants helps establish that level of trust, which in turn allows

for a rich and valuable exchange of ideas and sharing of personal experiences.  In addition to

trust and long-term commitment, action and personal accountability are necessary for

building sustainable EPL networks or programs (Brett et al., 2012; Collins et al., 2006;

Florén, 2003; Zhang & Hamilton, 2009).  Further research in this area is needed to better

understand (a) the roles of sensing and intuitive learning, (b) how entrepreneurs acquire and

make sense of external information in the learning process, and (c) what other social contexts

contribute to EL and what processes support or inhibit learning in these contexts.

So far, I have discussed the research and theory on EL from experiential,

organizational, and social learning perspectives.  I have argued that learning from experience

is a key aspect of EL and a fundamentally important ability in entrepreneurship, and that

critical reflection plays a major role in transforming experience into learning and

developmental outcomes for entrepreneurs.  I have shown that learning from experience can occur on multiple levels and can be either adaptive (involving changes to existing strategies for dealing with specific situations or types of situations) or generative (involving changes to underlying values or orientations toward self and world in general). I have also described how social processes contribute to learning pertaining directly to enterprise ownership and management, and pertaining to the underlying values and assumptions that inform the actions and choices of individual entrepreneurs.

As mentioned above, there is also a dimension of EL that encompasses identity, or learning about *who one can be* (Higgins & Aspinall, 2011; Rae, 2000). This dimension involves the construction and maintenance of entrepreneurial identity, and the discursive activities that support these processes. I discuss entrepreneurial identity development and the discursive activities that support it in the following section.

## Learning and Entrepreneurial Identity

How one defines oneself in relation to others determines how she or he makes sense of the world (Weick, 1995). Identity provides a frame of reference (Leitch & Harrison, 2016) for interpreting social phenomena and assessing potential actions and behaviors. In turn, the way individuals construct and enact their identities influences how others perceive them. From a sensemaking perspective (Weick, Sutcliffe, & Obstfeld, 2005), our notions of self-identity shape our actions and interpretations. This, in turn, affects how others view us and treat us, which either reinforces or destabilizes our identities. This reciprocal social process forms the background against which entrepreneurs construct and manage a sense of entrepreneurial identity.

Identities are created through the process of social interaction (Weick, 1995).

Therefore, one's sense of self shifts and changes in relation to various social situations.  In addition, the psychological need to present a coherent and consistent sense of self to others helps determine the shape the self takes from one situation to the next (Goffman, 1982).  However, as individuals define themselves differently in response to different social groups or situations, their sense of what is out there (i.e., external situations and circumstances) also changes (Weick, 1995).

From this perspective, entrepreneurial identity is as Leitch and Harrison (2016) described, "a complex, increasingly fluid, multi-level and multidimensional construct" (p. 179).  In the sections below, I first review the literature linking learning and identity, then discuss the construction of entrepreneurial identity and the discursive resources employed in entrepreneurial identity construction.

**Linking EL and Identity**

EL is about learning how to recognize and act on entrepreneurial opportunities, how to create and develop small enterprises, and so on.  However, it is also about acquiring identity, or about learning who one can be as an entrepreneur (Higgins & Aspinall, 2011; Rae, 2000).  Rae (2000) explained that in EL, knowing, acting, and making sense are interconnected.  Over time, as entrepreneurs put new functional knowledge into action, they further develop their understanding of what works.  As a result, they come to know that they "can do it," which influences the way they construct their notions of self-identity.  In other words, "People learn 'who they can be', construct stories of 'who they want to be' and work towards enacting their storied identity" (p. 151).  In this sense, learning *is* becoming, and is therefore integral to the process of entrepreneurial identity development.

Higgins and Aspinall (2011) adopted a sociocultural view of this phenomenon.

Drawing from Lave and Wenger's (1991) theory of "legitimate peripheral participation," they stressed that individuals acquire their social identities by engaging fully in the sociocultural practices of their communities. Culture, after all, provides its own resources for self-construction, delimiting the ways in which we may "legitimately conceive ourselves and others" (Bruner, 1997, p. 147). As a result, entrepreneurs can be viewed as developing their entrepreneurial identities by learning and participating in the social practices of entrepreneurship.

Finally, from a social learning perspective, learning and identity are connected *biographically* (Jarvis, 2009). Jarvis argued that the perceived content of learning is reconfigured through cognitive, emotional, and/or practical processes, and then integrated into an individual's evolving biography. In essence, "it is the person who learns and it is the changed person who is the outcome of the learning" (p. 24). Learning is thus fundamentally connected to identity, as it is the person who learns and becomes a more experienced person as a result of her or his learning.

Despite increasing interest from researchers, the link between learning and entrepreneurial identity requires further study. More research is needed, for example, that asks how the link between learning and identity unfolds in an entrepreneurial context. In what ways does EL occur and shape identity, and what social processes either support or inhibit this type of learning?

**Construction of Entrepreneurial Identity**

In the same sense that identity is acquired socially, the construction of entrepreneurial identity is also a social phenomenon. Entrepreneurs negotiate their identities through language and behavior, in relation to various circumstances and social situations, and within the social context of their communities.  This activity was defined by Sveningsson and

Alvesson (2003) as "identity work."  Identity work involves "forming, repairing,

maintaining, strengthening or revising the constructions" that result in a coherent and

distinctive sense of self (p. 1165).  Implicit in this definition is the understanding that identity

work is dynamic and ongoing.  Thus, from this point of view, identity itself is fluid and

changing, rather than static or fixed (Leitch & Harrison, 2016).

Identity work is also deeply embedded in narrative accounts of people and events, as

narrators construct their accounts in ongoing ways that position themselves in relation to

others (Watson, 2009).  Watson described these processes as "mutually constitutive,"

stressing that individuals strive to shape both a relatively consistent notion of personal self-

identity, as well as various social identities, "that emerge in relationship to others in the

various milieu in which they live their lives" (p. 257).  Identity construction is therefore a

relational or discursive activity—something that is accomplished through interaction with

others and through mutual participation in a common discourse.  It is also performative, in

the sense that identities are managed or enacted through social exchange in ways that adhere

to cultural rules and that attempt to fulfill personal desires (Beech, 2008; Goffman, 1959).

The subject of entrepreneurial identity has garnered significant interest from

researchers over the years.  However,  Leitch and Harrison (2016) maintain that more

research is needed which recognizes identity as a dynamic phenomenon, and which explores

the processes of identity work through which entrepreneurial identities are created and

managed.  What, for example, is the role of identity work in entrepreneurship?  What are the

processes through which entrepreneurial identities are constructed and negotiated?  How do

identities form and change in entrepreneurial ventures over time?

Insofar as entrepreneurs construct and manage their identities through social processes, they draw from cultural narratives (discursive resources embedded in culture and environment) in order to do so (Down & Warren, 2008; Watson, 2009). The cultural or discursive resources available to an individual under a given set of circumstances both shapes and constrains her or his identity construction and sense making (Down & Warren, 2008; Watson, 2009). The review explores discursive perspectives on the construction of entrepreneurial identity below.

**Discursive Resources and Identity Construction**

In the entrepreneurship literature, the relationship between discourse and identity has been explored from several perspectives. Broadly speaking, the conversation is about the linguistic constructs used by entrepreneurs to "establish, maintain, and convey a sense of an entrepreneurial self in everyday settings" (Down & Warren, 2008, p. 6). These constructs take the form of discourses or cultural conversations about entrepreneurship.

Rae (2000), for example, stated that entrepreneurs "learn the language" of entrepreneurial discourse through social interaction. In his view, entrepreneurial capability and identity are at least in part developed through the social process of learning the language used in the cultural discourse on entrepreneurship. According to Down and Warren (2008), this position rests on an understanding of language as "menus of discursive resources which various actors draw on in different ways at different times to achieve particular purposes" (p. 7). In other words, entrepreneurs use discursive resources in a context-dependent way, to position themselves in ways that suit their needs in specific situations (Watson, 2009).

Framed by this broad understanding, studies have explored the discursive resources available to entrepreneurs. One area of focus is the prevailing cultural discourse on enterprise and its role in shaping cultural notions of the "ideal" entrepreneur (Down &

Warren, 2008; Nicholson & Anderson, 2005). Another is the marginalizing effect that these

notions have on "non-normative" entrepreneurs (Mallett & Wapshott, 2015). Other

researchers have questioned the hegemony of a single normative discourse on

entrepreneurship, suggesting instead that entrepreneurs draw from a multiplicity of discursive

resources in creative and nuanced ways (Fenwick, 2002; Watson, 2009).

**Enterprise discourse**. The cultural discourse on entrepreneurship influences how

entrepreneurs negotiate their identity claims through social interaction (Mallett & Wapshott,

2015). Traditionally, this discourse has reflected the underlying assumption that

entrepreneurship is the engine of economic growth in developed economies (Watson, 2009).

As such, the received wisdom of enterprise culture is seen as privileging characteristics such

as individual responsibility, competitive individualism, self-sufficiency, and continuous

innovation (Dannreuther & Perren, 2013; Fenwick, 2002). Over time, the sedimentation of

these hallmarks of "successful" entrepreneurship has led to a cultural notion of the "ideal"

entrepreneur—a mythical or heroic and infallible protagonist (Down & Warren, 2008;

Nicholson & Anderson, 2005).

Cultural narratives of entrepreneurship have legitimized these notions by portraying

successful entrepreneurs as brave, ambitious, creative, risk-takers who thrive in conditions of

pressure and uncertainty (Down & Warren, 2008; Downing, 2005). However, the pervasive

and normative nature of this discourse causes problems for many entrepreneurs that don't fit

the mold (Mallett & Wapshott, 2015). In addition, the idea that individuals are beholden to a

single stereotypical ideal of entrepreneurship from which to fashion their identities (or fail

trying) may not be as accurate today as it has been in the past (Fenwick, 2002; Watson,

2009).

**Marginalizing effect of enterprise discourse**. In their qualitative study on the identity work of "olderpreneurs" (older entrepreneurs), Mallett and Wapshott (2015) found that the consumption of enterprise discourse and the construction of a coherent, legitimized sense of entrepreneurial identity are sometimes at odds with one another. Such is the case when certain groups (e.g., olderpreneurs, women and minority entrepreneurs, etc.) engage in forms of enterprise that run counter to the norms of the prevailing discourse. Excluded groups such as these may become marginalized, as they lack suitable discourses to draw from in supporting their identity claims. The resulting "narrative resource poverty" makes it difficult for non-normative entrepreneurs to overcome marginalizing discourses and the sedimented assumptions embedded within them.

Mallett and Wapshott (2015) argued further that individuals may exert agency in resisting the normative discourse—for example, by disrupting its rules (Fenwick, 2002). However, innovation of new or alternative discourses is limited by the available store of discursive resources which achieve legitimacy in the eyes of others (Mallett & Wapshott, 2015). In other words, in viewing identity as a social construction, marginalizing discourses shape others' views of what constitutes legitimate and plausible identity claims. Mallet and Wapshott claim there is a need to "support individual agency and claims for legitimacy through the development of new, counter-hegemonic narrative resources" (p. 15). One interesting question raised by this line of inquiry is whether local peer networks (i.e., peer learning or coaching groups) can help provide these resources—and if so, how?

**Multiple resources**. Although Mallett and Wapshott (2015) contend that enterprise discourse legitimizes only certain narratives of entrepreneurship while marginalizing others, they also explain that there is ongoing debate as to how much agency consumers of

entrepreneurial discourse have in the construction of their identities.  Watson (2009), for

example, challenged the notion that individuals involved in entrepreneurial activity are bound

within a single, encompassing hegemonic discourse.  Instead, Watson argued that

entrepreneurs draw from a variety of discursive resources and "institutionalized myths" in

their identity work (p. 268).  His single-case study of a growing family firm revealed how

two principal figures engaged with discursive resources related to strategic management,

family, and ethnicity—in addition to notions from enterprise culture.

These resources were used in creative, nuanced, and even contradictory ways as the

two actors negotiated their identities in a three-way conversation with the interviewer

(Watson, 2009).  An example of this is when "Ali," who on his own portrayed himself in

ways consistent with heroic mythology, later shifts in "Dina's" presence, abandoning the

hero when a better discursive position ("we ordinary street business folk") serves him (p.

265).  In Watson's view, the point of highlighting this exchange is to show that identity work

is relational and dialogic, and that entrepreneurs use multiple discursive resources, in

multiple ways, to make sense of what happens in their businesses, and to negotiate their

identity claims with others.

This position stems from the underlying assumption that entrepreneurs are "whole

people" and unique individuals first, before considering how their lives are influenced by

entrepreneurial work (Watson, 2009).  The "entrepreneurial identity" is simply one

discursive resource which individuals make use of in their social interactions.  Other research

has shown that individuals may exercise agency, resistance, and/or pragmatism in their use of

discursive resources to construct and negotiate their entrepreneurial identities (Down &

Warren, 2008; Fenwick, 2002; Storey, Salaman, & Platman, 2005).

***Exercising Agency.*** Storey et al. (2005), for example, stated that rather than passively absorb the discourses to which they are exposed, individuals actively "incorporate, modify, or reject notions of enterprise" through their reflexively organized self-narratives (p. 1050). Participants in their study demonstrated agency by manipulating notions of enterprise in order to judge themselves and their failures, to protect themselves from failure and rejection, and to re-classify problems in ways that validated their present realities.

***Exercising Resistance.*** In Fenwick's (2002) qualitative study of self-employed Canadian women, participants demonstrated ways of actively resisting competitive individualism, creating new models of enterprise and at the same time forging new enterprising self-identities. Many of these women were motivated by what Fenwick (2002) called "transgressive desires"—desires that transcend the traditional entrepreneurial discourse emphasizing profit, size, and growth. Examples included desires "to create nourishing workplace communities; to commit to sustainability before expansion; to honour 'right relationships' before competition; and to uphold ethical integrity before profit" (p. 717).

These desires prompted the women to break many business rules embedded in the conventional discourse (Fenwick, 2002) while defining their enterprises and their entrepreneurial selves. For example, a third of the women had not written business plans, and some reported setting their prices in ways that de-prioritized the maximization of profits. Others reported engaging in activities that did not contribute to business productivity, and maintaining interdependent alliances with would-be competitors. These actions reflect the participants' ways of constituting their entrepreneurial selves that resist the conventional discourse.

***Exercising Pragmatism.*** Down and Warren (2008) meanwhile, examined the

pragmatic use of entrepreneurial clichés as discursive resources for freelance entrepreneurs.

The metaphorical constructs of hero, warrior, explorer, wizard, or guru are commonly taken

up as resources for entrepreneurial identity management. However, these constructs

represent an oversimplified, gendered, and extraordinary version of entrepreneurial identity.

Down and Warren found that clichés (risk-taking, bravery, ambition, self-sufficiency, etc.) in

contrast, facilitate weak (breakable) attachments to entrepreneurial identities—attachments

that can be jettisoned quickly if things don't go as planned.

Given the unpredictable nature of entrepreneurial activity, these tentative connections

to entrepreneurship provided individuals with a means "to 'be' entrepreneurs without the

potentially compromising authentic commitment in their self-identity narratives" (Down &

Warren, 2008, p. 18). In this way, clichés may be adopted as "personal theories" (Rae,

2000)—analytical tools which help entrepreneurs determine what works (or what would've

worked) as far as interpreting and acting in a given situation.

**Summary.** Through the lens of identity, EL is about the construction and

maintenance of an entrepreneurial sense of self. In this section I have presented arguments

about the ways entrepreneurs construct and negotiate their identities socially, drawing from

various discursive resources. Some of these resources reflect a single hegemonic and

marginalizing cultural discourse on entrepreneurship, while others reflect the multiplicity of

discourses within which individuals are inevitably embedded. In addition, entrepreneurs

draw upon these resources in different ways at different times, in order to position

themselves in relation to others and to achieve desired ends. In the next section, I present several tentative conclusions from the literature on EL. I then review the literature on group coaching in order to help bring the setting for the present study into focus.

## Conclusions from the Entrepreneurship Literature

The distinct challenges of entrepreneurship make learning from experience integral to the entrepreneurial process. Yet learning presents its own challenges for entrepreneurs. Throughout the pages above, I have discussed theoretical and empirical perspectives on several learning-related issues presented in the literature. In the broadest sense, these can be organized into three basic types of learning-related challenges:

- Learning how to learn from experience

- Learning with and from other entrepreneurs

- Constructing and negotiating entrepreneurial identity

Together, they form a set of lenses used in the data collection and analysis phases of the present study.

### Learning how to Learn from Experience

Entrepreneurship is characterized by critical learning events. These events are often experienced as prolonged and traumatic critical "periods" or episodes, rather than discrete events with clear temporal and perceptual boundaries. While stressful and difficult to resolve, these episodes are influential in terms of facilitating learning and self-awareness. Learning in this context is fundamentally intertwined with action and behavior, as changes in perception and awareness lead entrepreneurs to act in new ways to resolve new situations that arise out of experience.

Furthermore, critical events or episodes can act as catalysts for higher-level learning: learning that involves critical examination of one's underlying theories of action, or the values and assumptions that guide her or his understanding of effective action. In an entrepreneurial context, higher-level learning is about learning how to learn from experience, or how to translate critical events and crises into learning opportunities. These activities require critical reflection: reflection that generates insight into the underlying values and perceptions that shape behavior.

Both higher-level (exploratory, generative) and lower-level (exploitative, adaptive) learning are necessary in entrepreneurship, but each requires a different set of skills and resources. While many entrepreneurs are proficient at lower-level learning—responding to changes in the environment, correcting problems, adopting new methods, and so on—learning in these situations rarely requires critical reflection. As a result, their underlying values and assumptions about action remain unchanged. In order for their enterprises to survive and develop over time, entrepreneurs must engage in critical reflection that leads to higher-level learning. An entrepreneur's ability to engage in critical reflection plays a key role in determining the learning and developmental outcomes of EL, and in negotiating challenges of this type.

Although much of the EL literature is grounded in an experiential learning perspective, more research is needed to understand how the entire experiential learning cycle unfolds in entrepreneurial contexts, how different social processes and contexts contribute to EL, and how entrepreneurs learn to develop the different sets of skills and resources required for both exploratory and exploitative learning. It has been recommended that research in this area explore questions such as, "What factors play a key role in EL at each stage of the experiential learning cycle," "what and how do entrepreneurs or entrepreneurial firms learn from the experience of other entrepreneurs," "what cognitive processes do entrepreneurs go through in different learning contexts," and "what and how do entrepreneurs unlearn?"

**Learning with and from Other Entrepreneurs**

All learning occurs within a social context. Learning is a collective process and a situated activity, shaped as much by sociocultural forces as by specific situations. Although EL depends on social interaction, isolation is a common reality for entrepreneurs and represents a significant barrier. Entrepreneurs often lack colleagues or peers with whom they feel comfortable sharing ideas, processing experiences, or even simply commiserating. Isolation stems from not having anyone with whom to discuss business problems, or in whom to appropriately confide. Since EL is both experiential and social in nature, isolation hinders one's ability to transcend the other two types of learning-related challenges. According to researchers, social contexts such as mentorship, peer networks, or peer learning groups can help counter the effects of isolation and foster EL.

In addition to reducing loneliness and isolation, peer interaction can produce a sense of universality, contribute new knowledge and ideas, stimulate critical reflection, and foster vicarious learning. Peer learning environments and other similar types of social interaction can proactively trigger reflection by exposing entrepreneurs to alternative perspectives, and by encouraging the questioning of ingrained behaviors and assumptions. In promoting higher-level learning, the role of peers is not necessarily to solve an individual's problems, but to help them clarify their thinking, consider alternative points of view, and resolve complex decisions. The value of peer learning is enhanced by the fact that peer learning groups allow entrepreneurs to observe and reflect on others' experiences, which may lower the costs associated with experiential learning.

Within the debate on whether entrepreneurial opportunities are discovered or created, the challenge of learning with and from other entrepreneurs speaks to the roles of sensing (external) and intuitive (internal) learning. The research on EPL shows that the social processes involved in peer learning can facilitate both learning types; that is, learning that is external or concrete, and learning that is internal or abstract. However, more research is needed to understand the roles of intuitive and sensing learning, and to understand how social processes can either support or inhibit them. A key question resulting from this discussion is, how do entrepreneurs search for and acquire external information, and how do they make sense of this information through the learning process?

Furthermore, there are no studies that explore EPL or other social learning processes in a group coaching setting with entrepreneurs. Previous researchers have shown that group coaching can function as a sounding board for the discussion of business challenges, offering new perspectives and opportunities to learn from others (Van Dyke, 2012, 2014); and as a source of managerial skills development (Scamardo & Harnden, 2007). These results demonstrate that group coaching is worthy of consideration as a potential learning and developmental environment for entrepreneurs.

Although some past research has concentrated on the influence of social processes on entrepreneurship and EL, the context has been either peer communities or community-based action-research programs. Group coaching may differ from these environments in important ways. Thus, further research is needed to understand how the social and experiential processes of EL unfold for entrepreneurs specifically through their experiences in group coaching. Therefore, another question arising from this inquiry is, given the influence of social processes on critical reflection and higher-level learning, how, if at all, do entrepreneurs experience the unfolding of these processes in a group coaching context?

**Constructing and Negotiating Entrepreneurial Identity**

Through the lens of identity, EL is about the construction and maintenance of an entrepreneurial sense of self. As indicated above, entrepreneurs construct and negotiate their identities socially, drawing from various discursive resources to position themselves in relation to others and to achieve desired ends. Learning-related challenges of this type involve the successful negotiation of identity, in relation to various circumstances and social situations, and within the social context of one's community. This is accomplished through identity work, which is the process of forming, repairing, and otherwise maintaining constructions that result in a coherent and distinctive sense of self.

Specifically, the challenges inherent in this work involve drawing successfully from existing discursive resources (learning the language of entrepreneurship), overcoming narrative resource poverty, creating new or alternative discursive resources, and learning to use existing resources in creative and nuanced ways. For some individuals, a principal challenge lies in overcoming the marginalizing effects of a prevailing discourse on entrepreneurship. They may do this by learning to exert agency, for example, by resisting and/or breaking the rules of the normative discourse.

The literature in this area leaves open key questions of import to the present study. Concerning learning and identity, for example, how does this link between them unfold in an entrepreneurial context? In what ways does EL occur and shape identity, and what social processes either support or inhibit this type of learning? With regard to identity work in entrepreneurship, what are the processes through which entrepreneurial identities are constructed and negotiated? How do identities form and change in entrepreneurial ventures over time? Finally, where group coaching is concerned, how does "coming in from the cold" and engaging with peers in a coaching context influence group members' constructions of entrepreneurial identity? What discursive resources does the group make available to its members, and how are those resources acquired? How do group members make sense of their participation in group coaching—specifically in relation to the construction and maintenance of their own entrepreneurial identities over time?

In the next section I review the literature on group coaching, including the characteristics of group coaching environments, the group-specific learning and change mechanisms at play in group coaching, and the storied experiences of group members.

### Group Coaching

As stated above, coaching is a multidisciplinary approach to facilitating learning and change that has roots in psychology, adult learning, and organizational development. The International Coach Federation (ICF) defines coaching as "partnering with clients in a thought-provoking and creative process that inspires them to maximize their personal and professional potential" ("Coaching FAQs," n.d.). Others have defined coaching as a process that supports the achievement of specific personal or professional objectives (Grant, 2006; Kilburg, 1996; Stern, 2004), and as a process that facilitates personal reflection and meaning making (Stelter, 2012, 2014). For the purpose of this study, I define coaching as, *a process that supports personal reflection and meaning making, as well as the achievement of specific personal or professional objectives*. The emergent subdiscipline of group coaching is concerned with the application of coaching principles in group settings.

Despite a recent upsurge in the number of theoretical works and empirical studies on dyadic (one-on-one) coaching (Grant, 2009, May; Passmore & Fillery-Travis, 2011), knowledge of the subdiscipline of group coaching is still in its infancy (O'Connor & Cavanagh, 2017; Stelter et al., 2011; Van Dyke, 2012).  As a result, the literature base is limited, and conceptions of group coaching differ according to a variety of theoretical perspectives.  Group coaching *includes* the coaching of intact work teams in organizations (team coaching), as well as coaching that involves other types of groups that may or may not have an organizational focus (Brown & Grant, 2010; Thornton, 2010).  To date, researchers have given more attention to the study of organizational team coaching than to other types of coaching groups.  However, in its latter form group coaching is becoming increasingly popular among practitioners and consumers (Britton, 2013; Ward, 2008).

There are no studies that specifically explore individual entrepreneurs' experiences of coming in from the cold, or wrestling with issues and challenges related to learning and identity in the context of a group coaching program.  However, the literature does help illuminate the setting for the present study, by discussing common characteristics of group coaching environments.  In addition, several texts serve to illuminate the group-specific learning and change mechanisms at play in group coaching environments (Kets de Vries, 2014; Stelter et al., 2011; Thornton, 2010), while others have explored the storied experiences of participants (Stelter, 2012; Van Dyke, 2012).  This section explores these aspects of the group coaching literature, following a brief definition of the term *group coaching*.

**Group Coaching: Definition and Context**

Multiple and conflicting definitions of group coaching appear in the literature. This state of confusion stems from the fact that the term is sometimes used to describe both a broad category or class of modalities (as above) and an item within that class (i.e., group, as opposed to peer or team, coaching). In addition, there is no consensus on what constitutes group coaching, or on what parameters are appropriate for distinguishing group coaching from other group-level interventions.

For the purposes of this study, I define *group coaching* as (a) the application of coaching principles to a small group, (b) across multiple sessions, (c) facilitated by a skilled professional, and (d) in service of individual, collective, personal, and/or organizational learning and goals. This definition, while still very broad, excludes several examples of group-level activities or interventions that are represented as group coaching in the literature.

Green, Oades, and Grant (2006), for example, conducted a study on the effects of a 10-week cognitive-behavioral life coaching group program on 28 adults, and found an increase in well-being, goal striving, and hope for group participants. However, their methodology involved a combination of large group workshops and peer-coaching conversations conducted in pairs. Based on the definition above, this type of intervention does not constitute group coaching due to the size of the group, the dyadic (paired) coaching, and the lack of skilled professionals to facilitate the coaching exchanges.

Similarly, Barrett (2006) studied the effects of group coaching on the health and effectiveness of 42 members of an executive team. His findings showed that group coaching reduced burnout, but did not affect productivity. However, Barrett's methodology involved a single-day facilitated large group session, followed by telephone and email follow-up contacts with individuals as necessary. This type of intervention does not satisfy the above definition of group coaching, due to the large group size, single-day format, and lack of small group interaction.

Kets de Vries (2005, 2011, 2014), Ward (2008), and Florent-Treacy (2009) have written extensively about psychodynamic group coaching in the context of organizational leadership groups or teams. Referred to as Leadership Group Coaching (Kets de Vries, 2005, 2011, 2014), or Psychodynamic Group Leadership Coaching (PGLC; Ward, 2008), these approaches were developed as part of an executive program at the INSEAD School of Business. However, the coaching interventions described by these authors utilize a short-term, single-day or 2-day workshop design. An orientation toward quick results—"change in a single session"—is, in fact, portrayed as a key characteristic of PGLC (Ward, 2008, p. 73). Florent-Treacy (2009), meanwhile, described small group sessions in which group members are coached by their peers in the program, as well as a single leadership 360° group coaching day facilitated by a trained executive coach.

Fusco, O'Riordan, and Palmer (2015) conducted an intervention that comes close to satisfying the definition of group coaching used above. Their format engaged small peer groups over three coaching sessions facilitated by the authors themselves. However, the coaching methodology they describe appears mostly to involve a combination of training and facilitation, supplemented by peer-to-peer coaching.

The aim of the present study is to explore the experiences of independent entrepreneurs (not affiliated with the same organization) who come together as a group and engage a professional coach for the purpose of advancing their individual knowledge and capability as business owners. Other examples of "unaffiliated" group coaching in this vein might include (a) a group of graduate students working with a coach to make faster progress on their individual dissertations, (b) a group of single parents who work with a coach to help

them navigate the challenges of parenting, or (c) a group of senior managers from different

companies (or different functional areas of the same company) who engage a coach to help

them develop their leadership and/or problem-solving skills.

O'Connor and Cavanagh (2017) pointed out that this type of group can benefit

members in multiple ways. For example, a coach can help individuals in the group draw

from the challenges, learning, and experience of the other group members. New

"relationships and understandings" can emerge out of group interaction, linking individuals

across their different situations and contexts. These relational learning and change factors

are not possible in dyadic coaching.

**Examples.** A search of the coaching literature revealed four examples of studies

focused on unaffiliated group settings similar to those described above. Van Dyke's (2012)

study explored the experiences of 21 executives who participated in 19 different virtual

group coaching programs. Her findings indicated that participants used their coaching

groups as structures of accountability, as sounding boards for the discussion of business

challenges, and as opportunities to gain perspective and learn from others.

Stelter et al. (2011) conducted a mixed-methods study on group coaching for young

people who participate in elite sports. Their study found that group coaching facilitated

social support measured in terms of social recovery. This resulted in the formation of

durable social networks and the cultivation of social capital among group members.

Whitley's (2013) action research study explored how group coaching can be designed

to support and facilitate lifestyle changes in people with long-term health conditions (LTC).

Five group coaching sessions were conducted with six individuals over an 8-week period.

The sessions were designed to facilitate interaction between group members, SMART goal setting and subsequent action, and the development of a supportive peer environment in which participants could reflect on their experiences. Participants reported that the group helped them practice the skills needed to achieve their goals, thereby supporting them to make changes in their lives, and to cope with and manage their health conditions.

Finally, Scamardo and Harnden (2007) implemented group coaching for managers as part of an employee assistance program (EAP) at the University of Texas at Austin. Participants reported that the group helped them achieve their individual goals for management skills development, while also providing some of the psychotherapeutic benefits of group work discussed by Yalom (1995), including universality, altruism, and the installation of hope.

Other researchers have focused on the coaching of intact work teams within larger organizations—either by external coaches (Hackman & Wageman, 2005; Hauser, 2012) or internal managers (Fournies, 1987; Rousseau, Aubé, & Tremblay, 2013). Although the coaching of unaffiliated groups may appear to have much in common with organizational team coaching, their differences are also important. These differences are outlined in Table 1.

Table 1

*Unaffiliated Group vs. Work Team Coaching*

| Characteristics | Unaffiliated groups | Work teams | Noted by |
|---|---|---|---|
| Focus | Individual goals and objectives | Team-level goals shared by all team members | (Britton, 2010, 2013; Cockerham, 2011) |
| Relationships | Bounded by the coaching agreement | Pre-established (co-workers or team members in the same organization) | (Britton, 2010, 2013) |
| Setting | Diverse—not necessarily organizational or business-focused | Organizational—within a single organization | (Britton, 2010, 2013; Cockerham, 2011) |
| Approach | Horizontal—comparable vocational levels; no hierarchically senior team leader or manager | Vertical—process focuses upward toward team leader's goals | (Van Dyke, 2012, 2014) |

In some cases the literature reflects a more porous boundary between these two coaching contexts. For example, the high school students who participated in the study by Stelter et al. (2011) belonged to the same school. Thus, it is reasonable to believe that they may have had pre-existing relationships before the beginning of their coaching program. Yet clearly they did not belong to the same work team, and the focus of the coaching was on their individual development.

Likewise, the managers in Scamardo and Harnden's (2007) study all worked for a single organization, but the focus of the coaching was on individual skill development, not on team or organizational goals; and the group members served at comparable vocational levels. Thus, the groups reflected a horizontal approach to group coaching, rather than vertical. In a vertical approach, the coaching process focuses upward toward a hierarchically superior team

leader's goals (Van Dyke, 2012, 2014). In these cases, it is difficult to classify the groups as

unaffiliated. However, they were not affiliated in the same sense as intact organizational

work teams, where the coaching is far more apt to be focused on team or organizational

objectives, and where the approach is almost certain to be vertical rather than horizontal.

**Group-Based Learning and Change Mechanisms**

This study is concerned with how entrepreneurs experience navigating their

individual challenges related to learning and identity in a group coaching context. I have

defined group coaching and its context for the purposes of this study. I will now explore

several ways of conceptualizing the impact of this form of group coaching on individual

learning and change.

There is no single, unifying theoretical perspective on group coaching. Approaches

mentioned in the literature draw from, and in some cases integrate, multiple philosophical

orientations. These approaches are supported by a combination of practical, theoretical, and

research-based knowledge. Orientations toward group-based learning and change vary

depending on the approach used, and each orientation brings its own key mechanisms of

learning and change. These mechanisms are likely to shape or influence the activities and

conversations in which group members engage, as well as the nature of their experiences in

group coaching.

In Table 2 below, I present four prominent approaches to group coaching and some of

their key mechanisms for learning and change. I then discuss these approaches in detail. The

first two, Learning Group Coaching (Thornton, 2010) and Leadership Group Coaching (Kets

de Vries, 2005, 2011, 2014), draw heavily from the literatures on group dynamics and group psychotherapy (Foulkes, 1948; Yalom, 1995; Yalom & Leszcz, 2005). Thus, there is significant overlap in the discussion between these two approaches.

A complete list of all the learning and change mechanisms that inform them is beyond the scope of this review. I have selected the following concepts based on their relevance to the present inquiry, and/or because they echo important themes and distinctions discussed earlier in the context of entrepreneurial peer learning. Other group psychotherapeutic factors, such as an emphasis on the here-and-now (Yalom & Leszcz, 2005) or on the enactment of social routines and social distortions in groups (Kets de Vries, 2014; Thornton, 2010), are not discussed in the context of entrepreneurial peer learning, but do appear in psychodynamic and group analytic approaches to group coaching.

Table 2

*Prominent Approaches in Group Coaching*

| Approach | Orientation | Key mechanisms for learning and change |
|---|---|---|
| Learning Group Coaching (Thornton, 2010) | Psychoanalytic theory (Winnicott, 1971), group analytic theory (Foulkes, 1948, 1990), group psychotherapeutic factors (Yalom, 1995) | Holding and exchange<br><br>Connectedness and belonging<br><br>Interpersonal learning |
| Leadership Group Coaching (Kets de Vries, 2005, 2011, 2014) | Psychodynamic theory, group dynamics (Bion, 1961; Foulkes, 1948), and group psychotherapeutic factors | The clinical paradigm—exploration unconscious forces affecting behavior<br><br>Recognition and resolution of maladaptive patterns<br><br>Mutual identification<br><br>Vicarious learning<br><br>Imparting information<br><br>Altruism |
| GROUP model (Brown & Grant, 2010) | Dialogue (Scharmer, 2009), progressive developmental group theory (Tuckman, 1965) | Goal focus<br><br>Understanding others<br><br>Performing |
| Narrative-Collaborative Group Coaching (Stelter et al., 2011) | Social constructionism (Berger & Luckmann, 1966), narrative psychology (Bruner, 1990), communities of practice (Lave & Wenger, 1991) | Focus on values<br><br>Collaborative meaning-making<br><br>Narrative unfolding |

**Learning Group Coaching (Thornton, 2010).** In learning group coaching, group members come together for the purpose of individual learning. Thornton (2010) draws from psychoanalytic theory (Winnicott, 1971), group analytic theory (Foulkes, 1948, 1990), and group psychotherapeutic theory (Yalom, 1995) in her discussion of the mechanisms that facilitate learning and change in this type of coaching group. These include holding and exchange, connectedness and belonging, and interpersonal learning.

*Holding and exchange.* According to Thornton (2010), "All coaching is founded in a developmental relationship blending enough safety in the relationship to enable an encounter with new information" (p. 28). The potential for deep learning and change though group coaching is fundamentally connected to the coach's ability to create a safe, trusting, and intimate group environment (Kets de Vries, 2011; Thornton, 2010). Such an environment allows for meaningful dialogue, and fosters interdependence among group members (Cockerham, 2011).

Thornton (2010) explained this principle using two terms from psychoanalytic and group analytic theory—*holding* and *exchange*. The term "holding" was coined by Winnicott (1971), and represents the nurturing relationship that forms between mother and infant. A holding environment is the space of trust and safety that arises out of this nurturing relationship. Winnicott argued that the creation of a holding environment is integral to the practice of psychotherapy, and that holding environments can be constructed through the interaction between therapist and client.

When an environment of sufficient safety is created in a coaching relationship, it allows for an encounter with something new. Thornton (2010) labeled this type of encounter as *exchange*—a term borrowed from group analytic theory (Foulkes, 1948, 1986). Thornton

(2010) explained that there can be no change and development without an encounter with difference, or something that is new or unknown. At the same time, individuals must be able to stand on safe ground when they are challenged by exchange. Consequently, one can only engage with difference (exchange) in an environment of relative safety and trust (holding).

Thornton (2010) argued that these two principles of holding and exchange constitute the basis for effective learning in dyadic coaching. In groups however, holding and exchange become even more complex. An effective group coach must create a holding environment large enough for multiple people, must be able to process difficult feelings that arise for group members, and must create sufficient safety for group members to engage in the risks associated with learning. At a group level, exchange is characterized by a multiplicity of perspectives and assumptions, and requires a "continuous iterative process" (p. 40) of absorbing new information and its implications.

***Connectedness and belonging.*** Thornton (2010) explained that connectedness and belonging are closely linked with the concept of holding. Groups that are "well-held" enable members to feel connected to one another and exude a sense of forward progress. The concept is also closely related to what Yalom and Leszcz (2005) referred to as group cohesiveness— "the attraction that members have for their group and for the other members" (p. 75). Members of a cohesive group convey mutual acceptance and support, and are likely to form meaningful relationships with one another, as well as positive regard for the group and its work (Thornton, 2010). This state of connectedness and the accompanying feeling of belonging act as a major catalyst for change (Kets de Vries, 2014). As Thornton (2010) explained, identification with a "good" group is experienced as a benefit in itself, while also boosting positive self-regard, confidence, and self-acceptance.

*Interpersonal learning.* A coaching group offers an ideal platform for reflecting on one's behavior and behavioral patterns (Kets de Vries, 2014; Thornton, 2010). Interpersonal learning takes place through the real-time enactment of social routines in the group, coupled with an intention to notice and observe these routines in order to deconstruct them (Yalom & Leszcz, 2005). This provides group members with opportunities to become aware of their behavioral patterns in relation to others (Thornton, 2010), to observe and develop a range of alternatives, and to experiment with different ways of doing things (Kets de Vries, 2014).

**Leadership Group Coaching (Kets de Vries, 2005, 2011, 2014).** As mentioned above, this integrative approach was developed as part of an executive program at the INSEAD School of Business. Leadership group coaching incorporates elements of motivational interviewing (Miller & Rollnick, 2002), group dynamics (Bion, 1961; Foulkes, 1948; Lewin & Lewin, 1948; Tuckman & Jensen, 1977), and group psychotherapy (Yalom & Leszcz, 2005). Of particular interest to this study are the following concepts: the "clinical paradigm," recognition and resolution of maladaptive patterns, mutual identification, vicarious learning, imparting information, and altruism.

*The clinical paradigm.* Kets de Vries (2011) argued, "a purely cognitive, rational-structural perspective… will be incomplete if it fails to acknowledge unconscious dynamics that affect human behavior" (p. xvi). The clinical paradigm (or psychodynamic lens) provides a way of viewing human phenomena and people's inner worlds. Through a clinical lens, people's behaviors and behavioral patterns are viewed as the result of unconscious forces that are hidden from view (Kets de Vries, 2014). Surfacing these forces can help group members explore the underlying reasons why they have behaved in particular ways under certain circumstances.

***Recognition and resolution of maladaptive patterns.*** From this perspective, understanding recurring themes and patterns requires looking into the past, and especially at early attachment relationships (Kets de Vries, 2014). A goal of psychodynamic group coaching is to become aware of how present relationships are affected by unresolved and maladaptive patterns formed during these early relationships. Developing this awareness helps group members adapt their behaviors in ways that serve them in the present.

***Mutual identification.*** Kets de Vries (2014) explained that while listening to the stories of others, participants "may come to realize that they are not alone… and that others… struggle with similar problems" (p. 89). In the group psychotherapy literature, this phenomenon is called "universality" (Yalom & Leszcz, 2005), and is defined as the realization that one is not alone in her/his struggles, and that others experience similar challenges (Holmes & Kivlighan, 2000). It has been demonstrated that participants in group therapy benefit from meeting people with similar problems, comparing their difficulties with others, and realizing that their own cases are not as extreme as they had imagined (Danino & Shechtman, 2012). Scamardo and Harnden (2007) found that the experience of universality helped resolve group members' isolation in a managerial context and temper their unrealistic self-expectations.

***Vicarious learning.*** Group members learn through observing and reflecting on others' experiences (Kets de Vries, 2014; Thornton, 2010). In a comparative study of the therapeutic factors of group and individual treatment, Holmes and Kivlighan (2000) found that individuals experienced the therapy of other group members—both through observation and through direct participation. More recently, Kivlighan (2011) found that individuals experience greater session depth when other group members engage in vicarious learning.

*Imparting information.* Occasionally group members may benefit from receiving

didactic instruction, direct advice, or suggestions related to a specific issue at hand (Kets de

Vries, 2014; Yalom & Leszcz, 2005). This information may come from the coach or from

one or more of the other group members. Kets de Vries (2014) claimed that explanation or

direct advice from a coach can sometimes reduce anxiety and establish a sense of control in

the face of particularly unsettling problems. Thornton (2010) wrote that feedback and advice

related to a group member's specific dilemma invites reflection and thinking about next

steps. Such instances often become the subject of follow-up in subsequent meetings.

*Altruism.* Ironically, helping others can elevate one's own sense of value and self-

respect (Kets de Vries, 2014). Eventually, group members become invested in helping one

another, and come to profit from the act of giving to others—not just receiving from them

(Yalom & Leszcz, 2005). Scamardo and Harnden's (2007) findings echoed this notion.

Participants in their study experienced pride and a sense of reward from the act of

contributing to other managers. In addition, Yalom and Leszcz (2005) pointed out that group

work (unlike dyadic therapy or coaching) encourages *role versatility* by offering

opportunities for group members to alternate between the roles of helper and helped.

**GROUP model coaching (Brown & Grant, 2010).** Brown and Grant (2010) offered

a goal-focused group coaching framework for organizational contexts adapted from the

popular GROW model (Whitmore, 2009). Their model, called GROUP, begins with the

same three phases as the original dyadic model (Goal, Reality, Options). However, in a

group setting, two new phases—*understanding others*, and *performing*—are added.

*Goal focus.* An explicit focus on goals distinguishes this approach as an alternative

to the psychodynamic approaches discussed above. Citing Hackman and Wageman (2005),

Brown and Grant (2010) contend there is little evidence to demonstrate that coaching interventions focused on improving interpersonal relationships result in improved performance. Instead, they argue that group coaching holds under-utilized potential as an instrument for creating goal-focused change in organizations.

*Understanding others.* The understanding others phase of the GROUP model is based on Scharmer's (2009) group dialogue process. According to Brown and Grant (2010), the goal of this phase is to engage the group in a generative dialogue—the purpose of which is to expand individual and group awareness, and to enable systemic-level responses to client challenges. The term *dialogue* in this context refers to a "flow of meaning" (p. 39) in which participants, thinking together, come to embrace new perspectives and alternatives, and to explore new possibilities through conversation together.

Drawing on the work of Isaacs (1999), Brown and Grant (2010) make an important distinction between dialogue and *discussion*. Where dialogue requires genuine openness, a commitment to embracing uncertainty, and a willingness to let go of being right, discussion involves arguing in favor of a specific position, in a back-and-forth exchange. The coach's role in this phase is to help group members "suspend judgment, become more comfortable with uncertainty and ambiguity, to be open, to listen to others, and… listen to their own personal internal processes" (p. 40).

*Performing.* The fifth phase of Brown and Grant's (2010) GROUP model focuses on "action design and implementation" (p. 40). Individual and group actions are discussed in the group, which helps to ensure transparency and accountability. Brown and Grant note that the performing phase extends to action taken both within and outside of the coaching session itself. Thus, actions taken in-between sessions are evaluated in subsequent sessions as part of an ongoing and iterative learning process. A variant of the GROUP model called RE-GROUP is used to incorporate these sessions, when action steps from previous sessions are *reviewed* and *evaluated*, before group members establish new goals.

The importance of action and experimentation as catalysts for learning and change in group coaching has been widely noted (Britton, 2010, 2013; Stelter et al., 2011; Thornton, 2010). Stelter et al. (2011), for example, argued that group coaching shares much in common with communities of practice (Lave & Wenger, 1991; Wenger, 1999). Practice, as defined by Wenger (1999), is "a way of talking about the shared historical and social resources, frameworks, and perspectives that can sustain engagement in action" (p. 5). In a coaching context, the way that group members collectively talk about their challenges can influence their willingness to take action and their readiness for change (Stelter et al., 2011).

Britton (2013) emphasized the role of a group coach in creating a focus on goal-setting, action, and accountability. Implicit in this understanding is the notion that coaching (a) is incomplete without action, and (b) happens in between sessions as individuals take action to integrate their learning into their lives and work (Britton, 2010, 2013).

**Narrative-Collaborative Group Coaching (Stelter et al., 2011).** In the *narrative-collaborative* model of group coaching, the primary focus is on the generation and application of insights gained through the process of shared meaning making. The approach is founded in social constructionism (Berger & Luckmann, 1966) and narrative psychology (Bruner, 1986; Polkinghorne, 1988). Stelter et al. (2011) conducted their intervention along three dimensions (pp. 126-7): focusing on and reflection about values, providing opportunities in meaning making, and narrative unfolding.

*Focus on values.* Stelter et al. (2011) explained that the coaches in their study helped group members reflect on the values "inherent in their intentions, wishes, aspirations, etc., as guiding markers" for organizing their careers, education, and private lives (p. 126). The aim of these conversations was to help the athlete coachees reflect on and better understand the *why* and *how* of their involvement in elite sports. Furthermore, the aim of this dimension was to help group members gain a better sense of how their actions and ways of feeling and thinking connected to aspects of self and identity.

***Opportunities in meaning-making.*** Stelter (2007) argued that meaning-making is central to the coaching process. In their study, Stelter et al. (2011) had coaches work to surface their group members' personal processes of meaning-making formed through both experience and tacit knowledge. This work also involved highlighting the social processes of meaning-making occurring in the group dialogue through social negotiation and the sharing of narratives.

***Space for the unfolding of narratives.*** Storytelling is fundamental to meaning-making (Polkinghorne, 1988). Human experiences are organized and made meaningful through the telling of stories. In narrative-collaborative group coaching, the coach allows space for the unfolding of group members' narratives. As group members share stories with one another, and listen to each other's stories, they form a basis for collaborative meaning-making, shared values, and a sense of belonging (Stelter et al., 2011).

According to Stelter et al. (2011), the most significant impact of their group coaching intervention was on the experience of social support measured in terms of social recovery. This meant that participants learned to share their experiences, thoughts, and reflections as part of a collaborative dialogue, and to collaboratively form new stories about (reinterpret) challenging events and circumstances to convey them in a new light. In addition, the participants reported changes in behavior reflective of becoming more socially aware and integrated with their peers—even outside of coaching. This was conveyed through the formation of durable social networks and cultivation of social capital among group members.

**Participant Narratives in Group Coaching Research**

The dominance of the expert or scholar-practitioner perspective limits the existing literature on group coaching. In other words, much of what is written about group coaching privileges the view of experts in the field rather than the rich and varied lived experiences of group coaching participants themselves. This is reflected in many of the works explored above, with the exception of Stelter et al. (2011), who embedded a qualitative interview of group coaching participants into their primarily quantitative study, and Van Dyke (2012).

As part of their study on narrative-collaborative group coaching for young athletes, Stelter et al. (2011) conducted an interpretive phenomenological analysis of participant experiences. Six group coaching participants were selected for mid- and post-intervention qualitative interviews, organized around finding out how group members made sense of their participation. The data indicated that interviewees found the coaching helpful in terms of clarifying their thoughts about self, life, and athletic training and competition. The clarifying action was perceived to be the result of receiving support from, and hearing the reflections of, other group members. Participants viewed the coaching group as a community of practice, which presented opportunities to learn from the experiences and perspectives of others. As a result, Stelter et al. (2011) claimed they came away from the group with new and meaningful strategies for effectively handling challenges in both sports and life.

Van Dyke (2012) conducted a qualitative research study exploring the experiences of 21 executives who participated in virtual coaching groups. Categorical content analysis of participants' reported experiences revealed five major themes (p. ii): (a) business education, (b) group process, (c) group facilitation, (d) personal development, and (e) virtual community. Participants indicated that their coaching groups functioned as structures of accountability that helped them reach their business goals, as sounding boards for the discussion of business challenges and strategies, and as opportunities for gaining perspective and learning from others.

From a group process perspective, participants indicated that both group cohesion, and an atmosphere of trust and intimacy, contributed to creating sustained opportunities for learning and change. Also, the groups were perceived to function as support systems, as individuals developed deep relationships and a sense of camaraderie with other group members. These findings support the notion that one-off or single-day group coaching interventions fail to capitalize on one aspect of group coaching that participants consider valuable. The coach's facilitation skills were also noted as having a direct impact on the experiences of participants, but mainly in the sense of making things run smoothly, versus impacting on individual learning and change.

**Treatment of narrative data.** While these findings are important and begin to illuminate individuals' experiences in group coaching, both tend toward a more reductionist or paradigmatic (Bruner, 1986; Polkinghorne, 1995) treatment of participants' narratives. This means that in each case, many narrative accounts were examined for their common elements. These elements were then thematically categorized in order to present an overall view of how interviewees made sense of their experiences (Stelter et al., 2011).

As Riessman (2003) explained, thematic analyses of narrative data emphasize the content of a text—"what" is said, rather than "how" it is said. This allows for the reduction of complex and nuanced stories of human experience into more manageable thematic material that can be used in the development of theory.  However, thematic or paradigmatic approaches are not appropriate for conveying the uniqueness of a particular situation, how the situation came about, or the emotional meaning connected with it (Bailey & Jackson, 2003; Polkinghorne, 1995).

In addition, the contexts in which speech is uttered (cultural and institutional discourses within which participants' stories are embedded, as well as the relational context of the interview itself) are not usually examined.  As a result, narrative data are decontextualized in the above studies, thus limiting the complexity and richness with which participants' experiences are conveyed.  Missing from the literature are studies that emphasize (a) the contexts in which individuals' group coaching experiences are embedded, (b) the way that participants employ various discursive resources in their constructions of group coaching experiences, and (c) the full complexity, richness, and emotionality of human experiences within a group coaching context.

**Conclusions from the Group Coaching Literature**

The group coaching literature, though limited, offers knowledge and perspective on the different contexts in which group coaching occurs, its many approaches and theoretical orientations, and its key mechanisms of learning and change.  As mentioned above, the present study is concerned with unaffiliated coaching groups—groups that mostly occur outside of a singular organizational or work team context.  These groups are characterized by a focus on individual goals, relationships that are usually bounded by the coaching agreement, diverse settings, and a horizontal approach.

There is no single, unifying theory of group coaching. As this review shows, approaches draw from and integrate multiple orientations, including psychoanalytic and group analytic theory, group psychotherapeutic factors, dialogue, narrative psychology, and communities of practice. Different approaches utilize different mechanisms of learning and change, including holding and exchange, universality, interpersonal learning, goal focus, collaborative meaning making, and so forth, all of which were examined above.

While conceptual models of group coaching practice abound, empirical studies on the experiences of participants are few—especially in the context of unaffiliated coaching groups. Research shows that group coaching with a narrative-collaborative orientation can help individuals clarify their thoughts about self and life, learn vicariously from the experiences of others, and reinterpret challenging events and circumstances to convey them in a new light (Stelter et al., 2011). Virtual group coaching (Van Dyke, 2012) can serve as structures of accountability for executives, as sounding boards for the discussion of business challenges and strategies, and as opportunities for gaining perspective and learning from others.

Although no studies have specifically explored entrepreneurs' experiences navigating challenges related to learning and change in a group coaching context, the findings above may still hold relevance for the present study. In addition, they support many of the principles and findings described in the literature on entrepreneurial peer learning above. What is missing from the literature are studies that emphasize (a) the contexts (cultural and institutional) in which individuals' group coaching experiences are embedded, (b) the ways that participants employ various discursive resources in their constructions of their group coaching experiences, and (c) the complexity, richness, and emotionality of entrepreneurs'

lived experiences in group coaching.

## Conclusion of Chapter 2

This review of the literature situates the present study in the scholarly conversations

on entrepreneurship and group coaching. Relevant literature areas within these conversations

include the experiential and social processes involved in EL, the construction and

maintenance of entrepreneurial identity, and the mechanisms of learning and change involved

in group coaching. With this review, I have also illuminated several debates and gaps in the

existing literature, which provide a substantial rationale for this study.

## Focus and Significance of the Inquiry

In the preceding review, I argued that the distinct challenges of entrepreneurship

make learning integral to the entrepreneurial process, and that social interaction plays a key

role in entrepreneurial learning (EL). I further asserted that EL is characterized not only by

the acquisition of knowledge, but also by the acquisition of identity—which in a discursive

sense involves a marshaling of resources to suit different relational purposes at different

times. I showed that entrepreneurs tend to grapple with at least three types of learning-

related challenges: (a) challenges related to learning how to learn, (b) challenges related to

learning with and from others, and (c) challenges related to constructing and negotiating

entrepreneurial identity.

I established that social processes, including those related to peer learning and

identity work, contribute to entrepreneurial learning and identity development in important ways.  While researchers have begun to explore the impact of social processes on EL, further research is needed to better understand these processes as well as the social contexts in which EL occurs.  Group coaching represents one such context, and the intersection of group coaching and EL has yet to be explored.  Further research is needed to understand how the social and experiential processes of EL unfold for entrepreneurs, specifically in relation to their group coaching experiences.

The literature on group coaching is still in its infancy, and many texts have focused on establishing conceptual models of group coaching and/or on examining different mechanisms of learning and change that underlie coaching practice.  Very few studies have focused on what people actually experience in group coaching, and none have focused on the experiences of entrepreneurs.  I argued that there is a particular need for further research that emphasizes (a) the contexts (cultural and institutional) in which entrepreneurs' group coaching experiences are embedded, (b) the ways that entrepreneurs employ various discursive resources in their constructions of their group coaching experiences, and (c) the complexity, richness, and emotionality of entrepreneurs' lived experiences.

This study sought to explore the experience of group coaching as a setting for entrepreneurial learning and change.  The research question was

*Given the impact of social processes on learning and identity, what does it mean to entrepreneurs to navigate their learning-related challenges in the context of a coaching group?*

This question takes on added significance when bearing in mind the loneliness and isolation that are characteristic of entrepreneurial lives. To what extent (if at all) do these individuals experience "coming in from the cold?" To the extent that they do, what does this mean to them in the context of their challenges related to learning and identity? Applying an awareness of sequence and temporal flow, how do entrepreneurs experience that path (from isolation into group coaching space), especially in relation to their learning-related challenges? How, at what point(s), and to what extent do they acquire new discursive resources, or new capacities for critical reflection (for example), along the way?

# CHAPTER THREE: METHODS

This chapter outlines research approach and design, including methods of data collection and analysis, sampling strategy, validity, researcher reflexivity, and findings from the pilot study.

## Research Design

### Purpose and Research Question

The purpose of this research study was to explore the experience of group coaching as a setting for entrepreneurial learning and change. Although research has begun to explore the impact of social processes on EL, further research is needed to better understand the social processes and contexts that contribute to individual learning. Group coaching is one such context, and the intersection of group coaching and EL has yet to be explored. In addition, there is limited empirical research on group coaching, and existing studies of participant experience are rooted in paradigmatic orientations toward knowledge. This study emphasizes the contexts in which individuals' group coaching experiences are embedded, the discursive nature of narrative constructions, and the complexity, richness, and emotionality of lived experience.

The research question was, *Given the impact of social processes on learning and identity, what does it mean to entrepreneurs to navigate their learning-related challenges in the context of a coaching group?*

### Research Approach

All research is bound within certain assumptions about the nature of the world and how it should be studied. This study is rooted in a *constructivist-interpretive* research paradigm (Denzin & Lincoln, 2011), using a qualitative approach and narrative methods of

inquiry and analysis.  A constructivist viewpoint assumes that any understanding of the world

is necessarily a construction, rather than an objective reporting of reality (Maxwell, 2013).

From this point of view, meaning is understood to be subjective and varied.  The focus of

research is on interpreting the meaning that individual participants give to specific aspects of

their world and their experience (Creswell, 2009).

In general, qualitative approaches are suitable when the research goal is to understand

the meaning that participants attribute to specific events, situations, or other social

phenomena (Creswell, 2009; Maxwell, 2013).  Qualitative research emphasizes individual

meaning, and often seeks to render the complexity of lived experience (Creswell, 2009).  In

addition, qualitative studies frequently examine the social contexts in which human activity

occurs, as well as the influence of that context on the actions and meaning making of

individuals (Neuman, 2012).

Where research on entrepreneurship is concerned, recent works have established the

validity and appropriateness of narrative approaches for developing new insights into the

nature of entrepreneurship and the lived experiences of entrepreneurs (Hamilton, 2006, 2014;

Rae, 2000; Watson, 2009).  With regard to EL, for example, narrative methods have been

used to form new and more nuanced understandings of  how individuals develop

entrepreneurial capability through learning (Rae, 2000; Zhang & Hamilton, 2009).

According to Rae (2000), narrative is a suitable mode of inquiry for exploring the "living

theories" of entrepreneurship implicit in individuals' stories of experience, as well as the

cultural discourses from which these theories are formed.

Narrative is a natural fit for examining the human, social, and cultural aspects of entrepreneurship, as well as the ways in which individual entrepreneurs engage with and shape their social world, and vice versa (Hamilton, 2006; Rae, 2000). Much research on entrepreneurial identity examines the role of cultural discourses and "master narratives" in shaping the self- and social identities of entrepreneurs (Watson, 2009). Such explorations of entrepreneurial discourse require methods that engage participants in the telling of stories. As Rae (2000) explained, "If we are to understand the life-worlds… of entrepreneurial people, we need an approach which enables exploration of the choices they make, through the accounts they give" (p. 148).

Riessman's (2008) writing on narrative methods emphasized the meaning-making function played by narrative. When individuals experience "biographical disruptions" or discontinuities, they make sense of these events through storytelling. This perspective bears much in common with entrepreneurship researchers' conceptions of learning through critical episodes (Cope & Watts, 2000) or discontinuous events (Deakins & Freel, 1998), discussed above. For all of these reasons, a narrative mode of inquiry is well-suited for addressing the research aims and questions posed by this study.

**Narrative inquiry.** The terms *narrative inquiry* and *narrative research* are used synonymously throughout this study. A narrative perspective in research operates on the assumption that human experiences are organized and made meaningful through the telling of stories (Polkinghorne, 1988; Riessman, 2008). Narrative researchers explore the stories or storied descriptions of events that take place in the lives of individuals (Pinnegar & Daynes, 2007; Polkinghorne, 2010).

Narrative inquiries may lead to general knowledge about a phenomenon (knowledge that arises out of a search for common elements across multiple accounts).  However, they may also lead to knowledge of the uniqueness of specific situations, or of how and why a specific situation came to be (Bailey & Jackson, 2003; Polkinghorne, 1995).  In either case, data in narrative or storied form are special because of their ability to convey the richness and meaning of human experiences.  Polkinghorne (1995) argued that the storied linguistic form is unique in its ability to convey the complexities of human activity, encompassing temporal sequence, human intention, and both interpersonal and macro-institutional contexts.

What qualifies as a story in narrative research, as well as the methods chosen to study participants' stories, varies.  Different researchers use different strategies of inquiry and analysis, (Lieblich, Tuval-Mashiach, & Zilber, 1998; Riessman & Quinney, 2005).  These strategies break down along different ideological, epistemological, and ontological understandings of the narrative phenomenon (Clandinin, 2007).  In terms of analysis (see below), some approaches mimic more "objectivist" modes of research, while others take a more holistic and/or relational view (Riessman, 2003).  Choices related to methods of inquiry and analysis bear heavily on the outcomes of narrative studies.  Therefore, design choices in narrative research must be consistent with the study goals and philosophical orientation of the inquiry at hand.

*Fundamental tensions.*  The multiplicity of approaches to narrative research, coupled with a lack of consensus about the meaning of the term "narrative," has led to a number of fundamental tensions in narrative research.  Polkinghorne (1995) has helped to disentangle some of these, by distinguishing between non-narrative and narrative data, and by drawing on Bruner's (1986) work to distinguish between two different modes of cognition and their influence on narrative research. These distinctions are explored below.

*Narrative data.* According to Polkinghorne (1995), narrative data are set apart by their storied form, whereby events and situations are organized in terms of a conceptual theme or "plot." A plot carries a notion of temporal sequence, and provides contextual meaning by which individual events are configured into a unified and coherent whole. A story combines individual events and happenings in such a way that they acquire relational significance. Non-narrative data, on the other hand, are pieces of information which lack a sense of historical or future meaning (Bailey & Jackson, 2003) and which merely provide factual information that is devoid of relational or contextual significance.

*Paradigmatic vs. narrative reasoning in narrative research.* Polkinghorne (1995) argued that narrative inquiries can be divided into two groups according to Bruner's (1986) *narrative* and *paradigmatic* modes of cognition. Paradigmatic approaches in narrative research use classification and categorization in order to produce general knowledge of a phenomenon (Bailey & Jackson, 2003). The process involves examining stories for their data in order to produce categories from common elements across multiple stories (Polkinghorne, 1995).

In contrast, studies that utilize narrative reasoning emphasize the particular characteristics of specific situations and lives, the temporal context of human experiences, and the intentions and consequences associated with various actions (Bailey & Jackson, 2003; Polkinghorne, 1995). Whereas paradigmatic reasoning focuses on elements of commonality, narrative reasoning focuses on what makes each instance of human action unique and remarkable. According to Josselson and Lieblich (2003), the search is for "truths unique in their particularity, grounded in firsthand experience" (p. 259).

Whether a study is grounded in paradigmatic or narrative cognition carries implications in terms of both method and outcome. Analytic methods, for example, can vary greatly depending on a study's cognitive orientation (Bailey & Jackson, 2003; Polkinghorne, 1995; Riessman, 2003). Paradigmatic modes of analysis tend toward a more thematic and reductionist treatment of narrative accounts (e.g., a search for common elements across the entire data set) in order to produce general knowledge from the particulars of individual stories. Narrative modes, on the other hand, tend toward more holistic and relational treatments (e.g., an exploration of the particularities of a given situation) in order to produce a higher-order, storied understanding of an individual's experience.

While the tension between these approaches is important to understand and acknowledge, not every narrative study falls neatly into one category or the other. In practice, these distinctions are often blurred, and different approaches borrow elements from both cognitive modes (Riessman, 2003). The importance of mentioning it here is not to position this study as either paradigmatic or narrative, but rather to provide context for some of the methodological choices involved in conducting narrative research.

*Fundamental assumptions.* Rae (2000) emphasized the fact that life stories are inherently "subjective, socially constructed accounts in which the teller is both actor and narrator" (p. 150). Narrative researchers embrace this assumption, and the related idea that narrative data are co-constructed as part of a collaborative relationship between the researcher and the researched (Riessman, 2008; Riessman & Quinney, 2005). Narrative, in contrast to more positivistic modes of research, does not assume or seek to establish objectivity (Josselson & Lieblich, 2003). Instead, narrative researchers acknowledge their own reflexivity and transparently explore their active role in shaping the research outcomes (Bell, 1999; Kroll, 2015).

The aim of narrative research is "to create interpreted description of the rich and multilayered meanings of historical and personal events" (Josselson & Lieblich, 2003, p. 259). This involves looking beyond (or beneath) the material "facts" of a story, at the shape and significance of participants' selective renderings of experience (Josselson, 2006). Riessman's (2003) explanation succinctly captures this notion:

> Narratives do not mirror, they refract the past. Imagination and strategic interests influence how storytellers choose to connect events and make them meaningful for others. Narratives are useful in research precisely because storytellers interpret the past rather than reproduce it as it was. The "truths" of narrative accounts are not in their faithful representations of a past world, but in the shifting connections they forge among past, present, and future. (p. 6)

For this reason, analytical attention must be paid to *how* a story is being told, for *whom*, and for what purpose. What cultural discourses contribute to the story's telling? Why are events ordered in *this* way, as opposed to another, and so on. (Riessman, 2008; Riessman & Quinney, 2005)?

***Validity in narrative research.*** "Validity" can be a loaded word in interpretive research as it tends to be associated with more positivist approaches. In much qualitative research, validity is based on establishing the accuracy of a study's findings (Creswell, 2009). Qualitative researchers utilize a variety of methods to help ensure validity, including triangulation (using multiple, converging data streams), member checking (taking themes back to participants to check for accuracy), clarifying researcher bias, and using rich, thick descriptions to convey findings.

Neuman (2012), however, commented that qualitative researchers are often concerned more with "authenticity" than with validity. Authenticity, in this context, means "giving a fair, honest, and balanced account of social life from the viewpoint of someone who lives it" (p. 125). Polkinghorne (1988, 2007) argued similarly that validity in narrative research arises out of the believability or *verisimilitude* of a statement or claim. Validation, in this context, serves the purpose of convincing readers of the strength of a claim, and of its merit as a basis for understanding. According to Polkinghorne (2007), the kind of knowledge claims that narrative research makes are claims about "the meaning life events hold for people… [and] about how people understand situations, others, and themselves" (p. 476). Readers assess narrative research for the believability and trustworthiness of its claims, rather than for accuracy in any objective sense.

Narrative researchers recognize that storied evidence differs from numbered evidence or direct observations (Pinnegar & Daynes, 2007; Polkinghorne, 2007). The point of narrative research is not to determine whether life events as described conform to actuality, but rather to determine something about the personal meaning experienced by individuals (Polkinghorne, 1988, 2007). Storied evidence provides support for claims about personal understandings of human experiences. However, the descriptive value of storied accounts should not be fully ignored either. Lieblich et al. (1998) charted a "middle course" in approaching narrative texts:

> We do not advocate total relativism that treats all narratives as texts of fiction. On the
>
> other hand, we do not take narratives at face value, as complete and accurate

representations of reality. We believe that stories are usually constructed around a core of facts or life events, yet allow a wide periphery for freedom of individuality and creativity in selection, addition to, emphasis on, and interpretation of these "remembered facts". (p. 8)

Threats to trustworthiness in narrative research arise out of the fact that the storied descriptions of the meanings of events experienced by participants are not an exact reproduction of experienced meaning (Polkinghorne, 2007). The limitations inherent in language and personal awareness, the social intentions of participants, and the socially constructed nature of storied accounts, are all potential sources of disjunction between experienced meaning and storied description. In order to establish the trustworthiness of their claims, researchers must address each of these concerns. The principal task is to reduce the distance between participants' stories about their experienced meaning and the experienced meaning itself.

Riessman (2008) recommended that narrative researchers employ several strategies to ground their claims for validity. These include "reliance on detailed transcripts; attention to language, contexts of production, and… to structural features of discourse; (c) acknowledgment of the dialogic nature of narrative; and (if relevant) a comparative approach… [to interpreting] similarities and differences among participants' stories" (p. 193). In addition, Riessman noted that proceeding along a "methodical path," carefully documenting all procedures and knowledge claims, and practicing critical reflexivity, all contribute to claims for validity.

*Reflexivity.* Riessman (2008) defined reflexivity as "critical self-awareness about how the research was done and the impact of critical decisions made along the way" (p. 191).

This includes personal awareness of one's role as a constructor of knowledge (Josselson &

Lieblich, 2003), and direct acknowledgment of the fact that the researcher is an active

participant in the research process (Curtin & Fossey, 2007). A reflexive stance takes into

account the researcher's own personal background and experiences, as well as her or his

positioning with regard to gender, age, race, nationality, and other sociocultural factors

(Bailey & Jackson, 2003; Josselson & Lieblich, 2003). It requires researchers to be explicit

about their own personal biases, assumptions, and values (Curtin & Fossey, 2007). Narrative

studies are strengthened by the inclusion of a personal statement reflecting on these issues

and on the researcher's personal inclinations and characteristics that are likely to influence

the research (Josselson & Lieblich, 2003). I have included a personal statement near the end

of this chapter.

**Narrative Analysis.** The term *narrative* is used to describe both a type of qualitative

inquiry (discussed above), and a family of analytical methods used in the interpretation of

storied data (Riessman, 2008). Several typologies have been developed in order to help

distinguish and classify different narrative analytical methods. In particular, the works of

Polkinghorne (1995) and Riessman (2003, 2008) provide a useful framework with which to

position the current study in terms of analytical strategy.

First, Polkinghorne (1995) noted two primary types of narrative analytical methods,

corresponding to the two kinds of cognition (paradigmatic and narrative) described above.

*Analysis of narratives* employs paradigmatic reasoning and processes. Researchers collect

stories and analyze them in order to produce descriptions of themes that run across the

stories, or across the characters or settings that appear in different types of stories.

Paradigmatic analysis, according to Polkinghorne, is "an examination of the data to identify particulars as instances of general notions or concepts" (p. 13).  The researcher inspects

several stories in order to distinguish common conceptual themes which appear in all of

them.

The second method, *narrative analysis*, is based on narrative reasoning and processes

(Polkinghorne, 1995).  It entails collecting descriptions of "events and happenings" and

organizing them into a *higher-order* plot or story that is informed by theoretical knowledge,

context, and actual events (Bailey & Jackson, 2003; Polkinghorne, 1995).  In narrative

analysis, the researcher configures elements of the data into a coherent explanatory account.

The process involves a synthesizing of the data rather than a separation or reduction of the

data into their constituent parts.

Riessman (2003) outlined a range of analytical approaches, although elements of her

typology reflect Polkinghorne's essential distinction.  *Thematic analysis*, for example, places

emphasis on the content of *what* was said—the *told*, rather than the *telling*.  The process

involves collecting many stories and "inductively creating conceptual groupings from the

data" (p. 2).  Like in "analysis of narrative," the search is for common thematic elements or

categories that stretch across multiple stories, participants, and events.  Riessman noted that

the thematic approach views language as an unambiguous resource, rather than as a topic of

investigation in itself.  The relational context of the interview, and the cultural and

institutional discourses that inform participants' stories, are usually not explored.

In *structural analysis* (Riessman, 2003, 2008), attention shifts to *how* participants'

accounts are constructed in order to achieve strategic ends.  Thematic content is not ignored,

but an emphasis on narrative form introduces new possibilities for interpretation beyond the referential meanings of a text. Narratives are examined for the specific devices narrators use in order to accomplish communicative work.

Finally, *dialogic/performance analysis* (Riessman, 2008) refers to a holistic interpretive approach, which "interrogates how talk among speakers is (dialogically) produced and performed as narrative" (p. 105). Whereas thematic and structural models ask *what* and *how*, respectively, dialogic/performative analysis asks *who* (or to whom speech acts are directed), *when*, and *why* (or for what purpose)? As in Polkinghorne's (1995) "narrative analysis," careful attention is paid to the interactional, historical, institutional, and discursive contexts in which narratives are produced.

Although Riessman (2008) does not say so explicitly, *who* can also apply to the identity of the person narrating. This approach assumes a performative definition of identity and identity construction. According to this view, identities are dynamically constituted in social relationships and "performed" with specific audiences in mind. As a result, dialogic/performative analysis is useful for exploring the construction and maintenance of identity as a social/discursive activity.

***Choices related to analytical method.*** The present inquiry is a multi-faceted exploration of entrepreneurial learning and identity in a group coaching setting. As such, different aspects of the inquiry call for different analytical strategies. For example, questions related to how EL unfolds in a group coaching context are best served by a thematic approach to analysis (analysis of narratives). The goal of the inquiry would be to identify common themes across multiple accounts, in order to create general knowledge of the relationship between EL and group coaching.

Similarly, a thematic approach would be appropriate for producing general knowledge about navigating entrepreneurial challenges in a group coaching setting. A thematic analysis could also produce general knowledge about the path from relative isolation into group coaching space (coming in from the cold), and about the meaning that path holds for entrepreneurs. Here however, an added structural emphasis could help uncover how individual entrepreneurs accomplish the communicative task of conveying their own movements along their respective paths, or conveying the significance of events that unfolded along the way. This would allow the study to compare and contrast the narrative devices used by different participants.

On the other hand, a dialogic/performative analysis of how entrepreneurs experience the path from isolation into group coaching space could reveal the influences of various discourses (family, enterprise, culture) on participants' sensemaking and rendering of their experiences. Such an analysis could potentially shed light on entrepreneurs' acquisition of new or alternative resources used in the construction and maintenance of their entrepreneurial identities. It would also bring the researcher's voice into the analysis, reflexively exploring the ways in which narratives are/were co-constructed throughout the interview process.

The present study blended multiple analytical approaches to produce both general and specific knowledge. The question is about which analytical strategy moved to the fore (which became the lead), and which became secondary or supplemental? For example, the study could've led with a thematic focus on how EL unfolds in group coaching, or with a performative/dialogic focus on the construction and maintenance of entrepreneurial identity, and/or on the discursive resources acquired by entrepreneurs as they navigate their challenges in a group.

The pilot study (discussed below) gave me an opportunity to experiment with both narrative and thematic analytical strategies, and to resolve this choice. Having explored the appropriateness of different analytical methods in relation to the collected pilot data, and having compared the preliminary findings resulting from both analytical paths, I chose to lead with a narrative analytical strategy, and to use thematic methods to supplement and strengthen my analysis and findings. However, in keeping with Josselson and Lieblich's (2003) advice, I remained flexible and open to change throughout the study, rather than clinging tightly to a rigid plan.

**Design**

This study used a qualitative approach and narrative methods of inquiry and analysis, as described above. The section below outlines the research design and methods used.

**Semi-structured in-depth interviews.** The study utilized qualitative interviewing as the principal means of data collection. Interviews are well suited for examining personal meaning, lived experience, and self-understanding (Kvale, 2007). According to Chase (2003), "When we listen carefully to the stories people tell, we learn how people as individuals and as groups make sense of their experiences and construct meanings and selves" (p. 80). In addition, interviews are effective at producing deeper understandings of the complexities of individuals' social worlds, as well as the social resources (cultural, historical, discursive, etc.) that shape and influence how their stories are constructed and told. I describe the interview protocol and strategy, as well as the researcher's stance as an interviewer, in greater detail below.

**Participant selection.** The meaning of the term *entrepreneur* is debated in the literature and in popular use. Throughout much of the literature reviewed for this study the terms "entrepreneur," "small business owner," and "small- and medium-sized enterprise

(SME) owner-manager" are treated synonymously. The definition implicit in these texts

depicts owner-managers of small firms, who have an outsized financial stake in their

businesses, and who are the primary decision makers in their firms (Cocker, Martin, Scott,

Venn, & Sanderson, 2012). However, some researchers draw a clearer distinction between

entrepreneurial and non-entrepreneurial activities and settings.

For example, Wang and Chugh (2014) contend that an individual's attitude and

behavior with regard to exploring and exploiting entrepreneurial opportunities distinguishes

entrepreneurs from non-entrepreneurs. Opportunity exploration and exploitation are widely

acknowledged as central processes of entrepreneurship (Shane & Venkataraman, 2000).

Thus, they inform the fundamental activities of entrepreneurs. In line with this view, Wang

and Chugh (2014) proposed that entrepreneurial and non-entrepreneurial be taken to

represent ends of a spectrum, rather than separate sides of a polarity.

In popular use in the United States, entrepreneurship and small business ownership

are described in distinct terms. Entrepreneurs are often thought of as bringing innovative

ideas or product offerings to market, embracing new risks and the unknown, and focusing on

rapid scaling and high returns (Seth, 2014, September 25). In contrast, small business

owners are often thought of as working with known products or services, tending to focus

more on achieving stability or controlled growth, and on managing known risks. This study

focuses on the experiences of those who in the US might commonly be called "small

business owners" rather than entrepreneurs.

However, holding this distinction too tightly runs the risk of discounting the lived

experiences of some entrepreneurs. Nearly all of the participants in this study, for example, consider themselves to be entrepreneurial, despite the fact that several of their businesses tend toward the non-entrepreneurial end of the spectrum. Their claims to entrepreneurship are important constructs in their notions of self-identity and in their organization of experience. This mirrors my own experience in practice. Many small business owners, for example, must think and act in enterprising or entrepreneurial ways in order to survive. They must often learn to identify and exploit new opportunities in the marketplace in order to achieve and sustain success, even when stability is their stated goal. They must also grapple with new risks and the unknown as the environment moves and changes around them.

Therefore, my use of the terms "entrepreneur" and "business owner" more closely resemble their use outside of the US where the distinctions between them are somewhat less pronounced. Adopting Wang and Chugh's (2014) notion of the entrepreneurial spectrum, my research participants' stories place them at different points on the entrepreneurial spectrum at different times, though none can be considered non-entrepreneurial. In addition, all of the participants identified themselves as entrepreneurs rather than as business owners, and several described what they saw as considerable differences between the two.

*Selection method.* Purposive or purposeful sampling (Creswell, 2009; Neuman, 2012) was used in order to select participants and cases that met the study's criteria for inclusion. Two sets of criteria were used—one to determine whether group coaching programs were eligible for inclusion in the study, and one to determine whether individual group members were eligible.

*Criteria for inclusion of group coaching programs.* In order for their group members to be considered for inclusion in the study, the group coaching programs met all of the following criteria, consistent with the definition of group coaching offered in Chapter 2

above:

1. The program is targeted toward entrepreneurs and/or small business owners.

2. The program is organized around the application of coaching principles to a small

   group.

3. Group members engage with one another over time and across multiple sessions.

4. The program is facilitated by a skilled coaching professional.

5. Group members come together in service of individual, collective, personal,

   and/or organizational learning and goals.


***Criteria for inclusion of individual participants.*** In order to be included in the study,

individuals met the following criteria:

1. Participants must own and operate their own business or entrepreneurial venture.

   a. Ideally, businesses must have 50 or fewer full-time employees.

   b. Businesses must earn no more than $15 million in gross annual revenue.

The U.S. Small Business Administration (SBA; 2016) generally defines small

businesses as employing 500 or fewer employees, with average annual receipts of

$7.5 million. However, exact standards vary widely according to industry. As

this study is concerned with sole owners of "simply structured" businesses (Hatch

& Cunliffe, 2013), I adopted the 1996 European Commission small and micro

enterprises standard (Deakins & Freel, 2012) of 50 or fewer employees instead.

Since the study is not concerned with any one particular industry, I established an

annual revenue standard of $15 million or less. This figure is consistent with the

SBA's standards for the advertising, public relations, and business support

services sectors, as well as other sectors not specifically named.

2.  If a startup, the owner must have considerable financial investment at stake (not

venture-funded).  The study focuses on entrepreneurs who are independent

owners and who do not share stake in their businesses with a larger entity.  This

helped to ensure that all participants had exposure to the financial and related

risks that accompany entrepreneurship (discussed above in Chapter 2).

3.  Participants must have actively participated in an eligible group coaching program

for at least 2 months, and at least three group sessions over time.  In keeping with

the study's definition of group coaching, this limited the sample to only

participants who had at least had the opportunity to learn and change over time in

their coaching groups.

Individuals who did not meet the criteria were thanked for their time, interest, and

willingness, and instructed that the present study is primarily interested in exploring the

experiences of entrepreneurs who meet the preceding criteria for inclusion.

*Size.* Nine participants met the criteria for inclusion and chose to participate in the

study.  Of these nine, two participated in the pilot study and seven in the main study.  Data

from one of the pilot interviews were later added to the main study, bringing the total number

of participants in the main study to eight.  This was an appropriate number given the design

of the study.  It enabled me to pay close attention to the complexities of each individual's

social world, as well as the social contexts (cultural, historical, discursive, etc.) that shaped

and influenced how participants' stories were constructed and told.  It also allowed me to

write up the participants' higher-order stories as longer-form narratives in order to convey this level of detail. A smaller number would have failed to capture a robust enough variety of experiences, and would have limited my ability to draw meaningful thematic findings from across the entire collection of stories. A larger number would have risked becoming unwieldy for the reader.

Six participants in the main study were referrals from two different groups led by the same group coach. The other two were each referred by different coaches and participated in separate group coaching programs. A summary of the participants' ages, genders, years in business, coaching group affiliation (by coach's name), and lengths of time participating in group coaching is listed in Table 3 below in the order they were interviewed.

Table 3

*Description of the Participants*

| Name | Age | Gender | Years in business | Group affiliation | Length of participation in group coaching |
|---|---|---|---|---|---|
| Pierre | 51 | Male | ~20 | Naomi | 8 weeks |
| Eleanor | 71 | Female | 18 | Susan | 6 months |
| Belinda | 34 | Female | ~6 | Julie 1 | ~2 years |
| Ted | 40 | Male | 2 | Julie 2 | 8 months |
| Scott | 54 | Male | 4 | Julie 1 | ~4 years |
| Lynn | 43 | Female | ~4 | Julie 1 | ~4 years |
| Rigsby | 29 | Female | 5 | Julie 2 | ~3 years |
| Mila | 54 | Female | 11 | Julie 2 | ~5 months |

**Recruitment.** I recruited group participants through the groups' coaches. The initial recruitment strategy consisted of two steps. The first step involved (a) finding and contacting coaches who provide group coaching services for entrepreneurs, (b) determining whether their programs meet the inclusion criteria, and (c) determining the most appropriate method for extending an invitation to group members to participate in the study. The second step involved formally inviting individual entrepreneurs to take part in the study.

*Finding and contacting coaches.* I began by circulating a Colleague Recruitment Email (Appendix A) to my extended professional network and to associations with which I am affiliated, such as the International Coach Federation (ICF), the Institute of Coaching

Professional Association (ICPA), and the Graduate School Alliance for Education in

Coaching (GSAEC).  In response, two of these organizations (the ICF and the ICPA)

distributed research notices about the study to their members.  The ICF maintains a database

of members who are interested in participating in research and notified these members by

email.  The ICPA posted a description of the study with a call for volunteers on their

LinkedIn group page.

I also conducted an internet/social media search for coaching practitioners nationwide

who offer group coaching services for entrepreneurs, and I contacted the authors of popular

books on group coaching practice.  I assumed the authors might coach entrepreneurial groups

themselves, or they may have been able to refer me to other coaches who do.

Having found several interested and willing coaches, I determined whether the types

of group coaching they conducted met the inclusion criteria stated above.  Three coaches'

programs met the criteria.  I then worked with the coaches to determine an appropriate

process for forwarding or distributing a recruitment flyer to their groups (Appendix B), or

having me speak to their groups in person about the study, and so on.  The goal was to

informally invite group members to join the study.

*Formally inviting participants.*  After determining the best way to approach group

members and extending informal invitations (via recruitment flyer, their coach, or directly

from me, etc.), the next step occurred when interested individuals contacted me for more

information or indicated that they wanted to join the study.  I began by providing general

information about the study and its purpose, answering any questions, and determining their

eligibility.  I used a checklist (see Appendix C: Participant Setup Checklist) to help ensure that this information was provided to every participant. Other items on the checklist included

thanking the participant for his or her interest in the study; discussing potential risks and

benefits, informed consent form, and types of interview questions likely to be asked; and

scheduling the interview itself.

Once individuals indicated that they wanted to proceed as participants in the study,

and after their eligibility had been confirmed, they received the following documents either

electronically or by posted mail:

1. An Informed Consent Form (see Appendix D) confirming their participation in

   the study and outlining general information about the project.

2. An outline of the types of questions that were likely to be asked of participants

   (Appendix E).

I then scheduled the participants' interviews and obtained signed copies of the Informed

Consent Form before each interview took place.

**Data collection.** Data collection was accomplished via one-on-one, semi-structured

interviews with each participant. Six interviews were conducted face-to-face, and three

(including two pilot interviews) were conducted via Zoom web conference (audio only). The

interviews ranged from 60-96 minutes in length. Qualitative interviewing can take many

forms, and the term "semi-structured" can be used to describe a wide range of interview

formats. The interview protocol for this study was designed according to Kvale's (2007)

recommendations for conducting semi-structured life-world interviews, and Chase's (2003)

advice on interview questions in narrative research.

*Interview procedures.* Kvale (2007) stated that the semi-structured life-world

interview "seeks to obtain descriptions of the life-world of the interviewee with respect to interpreting the meaning of the described phenomenon" (p. 51). The interview format should

follow a sequence of themes that reflect the theoretical frames presented in the literature

review, with some potential questions that point toward each theme. However, it is

important to be open to changes related to the sequence and formulation of questions, in

order to follow the story as it is told by the interviewee.

Chase (2003) went a step further, advising students of narrative research to write

"lengthy, detailed interview guides" (p. 83) which reflect the anticipated conversational flow

of the interview. Then, apart from asking one opening question that invites a life story,

interviewers should ask only questions that "follow from a close listening to the narrator's

story" (p. 83) rather than adhering to the questions in their interview guide. According to

Chase, the purpose of writing an extensive interview guide is to prepare the interviewer to be

open to a wide range of possible stories from participants, and to cement a general awareness

of what the interviewer wants to know.

Kvale (2007) also commented on the importance of *setting the stage*, or establishing a

sense of trust and rapport, during the first few minutes of each interview. He recommended

that interviewers first conduct a "briefing" in which the interviewer "defines the situation for

the subject" (p. 55). The briefing should include stating the purpose of the interview,

explaining the use of any recording equipment, and addressing any questions that the

participant might have.

Applying these recommendations from Kvale (2007) and Chase (2003), I formulated

an interview guide (Appendix E) based on my discussion of the theoretical literature in

Chapter 2. I designed the interviews to elicit storied descriptions of group coaching

experiences that participants found personally meaningful or impactful. I began each interview with a briefing.  In order to understand the context in which these defining events occurred, I also asked the participants to tell me about how they became entrepreneurs, and about how they became involved in group coaching.  I directed the conversations away from participants' stories about their entrepreneurial histories and toward their stories about their group coaching experiences at around the 20- to 30-minute mark during each interview.

The interviews were mostly unstructured, with the exception of the prompts I used to move each interview through these three broad areas of inquiry.  As the participants related their stories, I responded with questions that clarified, probed, and developed the emerging storylines.  Kvale's (2007) typology of interviewer questions (pp. 60-62) aided in this purpose, as did Chase's (2003) discussion of question formulations that evoke stories of experience rather than generalities.  All interviews were recorded (audio only) and transcribed for analysis.

Given this predetermined structure of the interviews, most of them followed a similar overarching sequence of events in participants' lives, though not always in chronological order.  All of the interviews, for example, reached back into the past to explore participants' entrepreneurial beginnings.  This yielded rich stories of their transitions into entrepreneurship and the genesis of their entrepreneurial careers.  All of the interviews explored participants' stories about becoming involved in group coaching.  This produced highly vivid accounts of their experiences joining with other entrepreneurs, finding commonality and close-knit relationships with peers, and exchanging feedback and support.  The interviews probed participants' meaningful or defining moments in group coaching, which resulted in stories of learning and change and detailed accounts of the impact of these learning experiences.  Finally, a fourth component of the interviews involved looking backward from the present, reflecting on all of these past experiences, and reconstructing their meaning in the relational

context of the interview itself.

*Interviewer's stance.* In narrative research, narration is understood as having an

interactional or dialogic component (Chase, 2003; Riessman & Quinney, 2005). Narratives

are jointly produced, or co-constructed, by both teller and listener (Bell, 1999). Salmon and

Riessman (2008) explained that audiences, whether physically present or not, play a crucial

role in shaping what is and is not expressed in interviews, as well as *how*. In research

interviews, "the personal account… which has traditionally been seen as the expression of a

single subjectivity, is in fact always a co-construction" (p. 80). As a result, it is important for

researchers to maintain reflexive awareness of how they act jointly to construct narrative

accounts in their interviews. A more detailed discussion of reflexivity in this study is

included in the Researcher's Statement below.

**Data analysis.** Drawing from the discussion of narrative analytical approaches

above, I chose narrative analysis (Polkinghorne, 1995) as the primary analytical strategy for

the study. This strategy emphasizes placing stories within their wider relational, discursive,

and macro-institutional contexts. In line with Polkinghorne's advice and Bell's (1999)

exemplary analysis of women's health politics and DES survivors, such an emphasis lends

itself to the creation of higher-order explanatory stories about entrepreneurs' personal

experiences in group coaching.

My framework for narrative analysis was based on Riessman's dialogic/performative

approach (2008) and Polkinghorne's work on narrative configuration (1995). The process

involved the following steps:

1. After the interview data are collected, begin by listening to each recorded interview, all the way through.  The purpose of this step is to familiarize oneself with the data.

2. Then, listen again, while following along with each interview transcript.  On the transcripts, make note of each of the following:

   - Speech elements – including use of *direct speech*, descriptive *asides*, *repetition*, *expressive sounds*, and *historical present tense*.  These are all linguistic features of the performance genre which help convey the relational context of the interview environment, as well as the speaker's preferred self-presentation (Riessman, 2008).

   - Scenes – bounded segments of text, portraying unfolding action and its result.  Scenes, which often include characters with distinct speaking roles, indicate the speaker's choice of a dramatic presentation of her or his story, rather than a mere report of what happened.  Dramatic presentations are designed to draw the audience in, and to influence what the audience believes about the story, the characters, and the narrator (Riessman, 2008).

   - Contextual information – thematic material from other parts of the interview; as well as references to cultural, historical, and/or economic contexts, public discourses, and so on.  This information helps illuminate the broader context in which the narrated story is embedded.

3. Having marked the transcripts in this way, work to configure all of the resulting data elements into an over-arching and emergent plot or higher-order story of each interview (Polkinghorne, 1995).  The purpose of configuring the data in this

way is to organize and give meaning to the data elements as pieces of an unfolding temporal process.

4. Develop the stories further by citing specific quotes and examples from the data and connecting elements of the stories to the broader cultural/historical discourses in which they are embedded.

As mentioned previously, the pilot study offered an opportunity to experiment with both narrative and thematic analytical strategies and to compare their findings. This imparted me with a strong sense of how the two strategies could be used in concert to strengthen and inform one another. As a result, I chose to supplement the narrative analytical process described above with a separate thematic analysis of the data. Using thematic analytical methods allowed me to cut across the entire collection of higher-order stories that result from my narrative analysis, thereby strengthening my research and findings by making meaning of the entire collection of stories taken together. For my thematic analysis, I used the six-phase process defined by Braun and Clarke (2006):

1. Familiarizing yourself with your data – Listen carefully and completely to each recorded interview.

2. Generating initial codes – Read through each transcript, noting interesting and relevant features of the data to generate an initial set of codes.

3. Searching for themes – Search for potential themes across the data set and experiment with different ways of organizing the codes by theme.

4. Reviewing themes – Review and refine the themes.

5. Defining and naming themes – Create a thematic map of the analysis, and weave together an overall story of the analysis.

6. Produce the report.

**Validity.** As indicated above, validity in narrative research arises out of the believability or verisimilitude of statements or claims about personal meaning (Polkinghorne, 1988, 2007). Threats to validity arise out of the fact that the storied descriptions of the meanings of events experienced by participants are not an exact reproduction of experienced meaning (Polkinghorne, 2007). With regard to validity, the chief task for narrative researchers involves reducing the distance between participants' stories about their experienced meaning and the experienced meaning itself.

This study used the following strategies suggested by Riessman (2008) and adapted from Mishler (1986) to help ensure verisimilitude:

- Analysis relied on detailed transcripts of the interview conversations.

- Attention was paid to language, contexts of production, and (if appropriate) to structural features of discourse, including (a) the limitations inherent in language and personal awareness, and (b) the social intentions of participants (Polkinghorne, 2007).

- Attention was given to the dialogic nature of narrative, including the socially constructed nature of storied accounts (Polkinghorne, 2007).

- A comparative approach was used to interpret the similarities and differences among participants' stories.

- Thick, rich description was used to convey findings (Creswell, 2009).

- All procedures and knowledge claims were carefully documented.

- The researcher attended to and practiced reflexivity, including clarifying

   researcher bias (Creswell, 2009).

**Presentation of findings.** The use of multiple analytical methods resulted in

multiple types of findings, each reflecting different aspects or dimensions of the research

phenomenon. I handled this by dividing Chapter 4 into three distinct sections. The first

conveys findings from thematic analysis, while the third reflects narrative analytical

principles. Part 2 sits between them and draws from both narrative and thematic methods. I

explain this in further detail in Chapter 4 below.

**Data management.** All electronic communications, interview transcripts, and digital

recordings of interviews were stored electronically on the researcher's secure hard drive, as

well as on a secure backup external drive. All printed copies of electronic files and signed

informed consent forms were kept in a locked file cabinet in my office. The key connecting

participant identifiers with pseudonyms was kept on a secure, cloud-based drive separate

from the hard drive where all other research data were stored. At the conclusion of the study,

I will erase this key, along with all electronic communications and participant identifiers. I

will erase all other data files (including digital interview recordings and transcripts) and

shred all printed copies within 3 years of research completion.

## Protection of Human Participants

**Voluntary participation.** Participation in the study was voluntary, and participants

were notified of their option to withdraw from the study at any time without penalty or

negative consequences. At any time up until completion of the study, participants may request that previously provided information be removed from the study. Each participant

was informed about the potential risks and benefits associated with participating in the study.

All of this information was provided in an Informed Consent Form (Appendix D) and

reviewed verbally with each participant.

**Confidentiality and anonymity.** All responses and related study records were held

in confidence. Participants were asked to select a pseudonym to be used in place of their

name in the transcripts and in the research report. The key connecting participant identifiers

with their pseudonyms was kept on a secure, cloud-based drive separate from the hard drive

where all other research data are stored. Identifying references to participants' businesses,

coaches, or coaching groups were also anonymized through the use of pseudonyms.

Individuals' consent to participate in the study included consent for the researcher,

supervising faculty, and (if applicable) a confidential research assistant to review the data.

Research records may also be inspected by authorized representatives of Fielding Graduate

University, including members of the Institutional Review Board or their designees. The

published results of this research including the final dissertation, subsequent journal articles,

books, or professional presentations may include the use of direct quotes from interviews. In

such cases all identifying information will be removed. Direct quotes will be attributed to the

pseudonyms chosen by or assigned to participants. This information was provided to

participants by way of Informed Consent (Appendix D).

**Researcher Statement**

As indicated above, a reflexive stance in research takes into account the researcher's

own background and experiences, as well as her or his personal biases, assumptions, and

values. Since narrative research does not assume objectivity (Josselson & Lieblich, 2003), narrative studies are strengthened when researchers acknowledge and inquire into their own subjectivity. This often includes stating philosophical, professional, and/or personal assumptions and biases that have the potential to influence the research project. I discuss my own biases and assumptions about coaching and enterprise below. In addition, the narrative-constructionist orientation of this study calls for a deeper exploration of the concept of reflexivity—beyond the impact of personal biases and assumptions. This idea is also taken up below, and discussed in terms of (a) audience, (b) the notion of the "coaching interview," and (c) thinking about rapport.

**Biases and assumptions.** As a professional certified coach and organizational consultant who specializes in working with entrepreneurs in both one-on-one and group settings, I bring to this study a range of experiences and assumptions that are likely to intersect with this research project. First, anecdotal evidence from my practice has demonstrated that some forms of coaching, including certain types of group coaching, support and facilitate entrepreneurial learning and development. This has not yet been established through empirical research. In addition, I have witnessed the construction, evolution, and maintenance of entrepreneurial identity in many of my clients. It is my belief and assumption that my work with these clients has contributed to these processes in a significant way. These experiences may interfere with my ability to acknowledge evidence and examples to the contrary if and when they do appear.

Second, I bring my own biases about what does and does not constitute effective coaching and consultation. For example, I tend to view long-term engagement with clients as necessary for cultivating deep and systemic growth and change. Whereas, many in the coaching field would argue that an orientation toward short-term results is fundamental to effective coaching. I may inadvertently discount or dismiss possibilities for learning and

change as a result of a specific coaching program's design, orientation, or methodology.

Finally, my political and philosophical views tend to support models of business and

entrepreneurship that demonstrate social and ecological awareness and responsibility. I am

often critical of businesses that celebrate competitive individualism, exploitative or dishonest

business practices, and/or a "win at all costs" mentality. Particularly given this study's goal

of exploring the discursive resources that influence entrepreneurs' sense making and identity

construction, it is important for me to remain open to the stories of entrepreneurs who do not

necessarily share my convictions.

**Audience.** Given the narrative-constructionist orientation of this study, issues of

reflexivity go beyond acknowledging the influence of the researcher's biases and personal

characteristics. Narratives are constructed with specific audiences in mind. In the context of

my interviews, I am an audience member affecting how participants' stories are constructed.

Given that this is the case, it is important to think about how the participants relate to me as

an audience member, and how they construct their accounts in light of this. Who is the Erek

in the interview? Do they see me as a doctoral student? As a coach? As a friend of their

coach? Does this impression change over the course of the interview?

These questions were critically important to interpreting participants' discursive

constructions and storied accounts. Although it is impossible to answer them in any

objective fashion, Schön's (1983) work on reflective practice suggests that it may be possible

to maintain an awareness of this line of questioning during the interviews (reflection-in-

action), as well as through retrospective reflection and analysis (reflection-on-action).

**The coaching interview.** As I was a coach interviewing people about their experiences in coaching situations, the study also presented an opportunity to explore the recursive nature of the interview process itself. It was not my intention to approach the interview as I would a coaching session, or to coach my research participants through their interviews. However, by nature of the types of questions I asked, it is possible that my participants gained knowledge or insight from the interview process that closely parallels (or extends) the learning that they described retrospectively through their stories.

It is also possible that through our conversations participants learned something about *how* they learn in their coaching groups. I attempted to include these phenomena in the study by asking what was happening in the interview itself that was furthering this learning. The study presented an opportunity to embrace (rather than bracket or mitigate) these dynamics, and to explore the interview even as its own kind of coaching interaction—the "coaching interview" (F. Steier, personal communication, October 4, 2016). I was able to explore this issue directly during the interviews by asking how my participants made sense of what happened in the interview itself. As an entry point for this inquiry, I included the question in my interview guide (Appendix E), "What are you taking away from our conversation today?"

**Thinking about rapport.** Although it is common for researchers to think of rapport in an instrumental sense or as a means for acquiring high-quality data (Jorgenson, 1995), the notion of reflexivity explored here suggests that rapport should be viewed as a social or relational process instead. Jorgenson suggested that rapport arises out of "the situation between researcher and collaborators" (p. 167). Making this shift requires a reprioritization—an increased emphasis on interview process, and a decreased emphasis on interview content. Attention is paid to supplying the requisite conditions for rapport (empathy, social skills, sensitivity to others' experience, etc.), and to exploring (rather than

ignoring or suppressing) the divergences and contradictions that surface in respondents'

stories. Within these seemingly peripheral comments lie clues about the respondent's

identity construction.

Here again, a reflexive stance requires recognizing that the respondent's notion of the

interviewer is both (a) a social construction and (b) subject to change from moment to

moment. Jorgenson (1995) explains,

> How respondents construct the interviewer as a social type profoundly influences the
>
> form of their responses—whether they see her as a detached scientist, as a
>
> knowledgeable expert with valuable resources, as a critic, or as a comember of a
>
> particular social category… will shape their interpretation of her questions, and
>
> consequently, their responses. (p. 166)

To summarize, I have suggested several ways that issues involving reflexivity were

likely to influence this study. I began with an evaluation of my own biases and assumptions,

and then explored the notion of audience, the idea of the coaching interview, and thinking

about rapport as a relational phenomenon. A key principle underlying this discussion is the

idea that participants' constructions of the interviewer (a) can change from moment to

moment, and (b) hold major implications for data collection and interpretation.

**Pilot Study**

Pilot studies are conducted in order to test the proposed methods for a research

project, and to use knowledge gained from the test to make any necessary changes to the

study design. For my pilot study I conducted interviews with two small business owners who

participated in group coaching programs. The study offered a valuable opportunity to experiment with narrative interviewing, and to explore two different strategies of analysis (narrative and thematic) in order to compare and contrast their findings. In the paragraphs below, I discuss my preliminary findings from the pilot data, as well as key takeaways for improving the study and my skills as a researcher.

**Preliminary findings.** I conducted both narrative (Polkinghorne, 1995; Riessman, 2008) and thematic (Braun & Clarke, 2006) analyses of my data set. This enabled me to compare and contrast the two processes and their respective outcomes. Both analyses were aimed at addressing the same research question stated above: *Given the impact of social processes on learning and identity, what does it mean to entrepreneurs to navigate their learning-related challenges in the context of a coaching group?*

***Findings from narrative analysis.*** Narrative analysis of the pilot data indicated that group coaching intersects the life and business trajectories of entrepreneurs in both simple and complex ways. In the simplest sense, these group members found group coaching to be meaningful as a source of practical knowledge that helped them navigate common business challenges, such as identifying a target audience, developing a business plan, or accumulating wealth. Through their interactions with peers and coach, they also acquired a meaningful sense of commonality, and benefitted indirectly from opportunities to step into the coaching role themselves in order to help their peers.

In a more holistic sense, their group coaching provided an environment where they could engage in higher-level learning by identifying and interacting with their long-held beliefs and assumptions about themselves, about business, and about success. The data indicate that the participants entered into their coaching groups with long-standing notions about business and success, influenced by early childhood experiences and broader cultural discourses. Through their group coaching experiences, they were prompted to reflect on and critically deconstruct these lifelong trajectories, and to acquire new (alternative) resources which they used to construct new personal theories of self, entrepreneurship, and success.

The group environment helped legitimize these emergent narrations of self and business in ways that one-on-one coaching cannot. This is due to the fact that social support from peers was perceived to be more convincing ("they're not getting paid to tell you you're great") than from the coach alone. Also, some role versatility was present in the groups (group members provided coaching and feedback for their peers, putting them in the role of the helper), whereas the roles of coach and client are more rigidly defined in a dyadic coaching relationship. The interview process itself helped reinforce this learning by forcing interviewees to resurface and articulate what they had learned.

*Findings from thematic analysis.* Thematic analysis of the pilot data revealed a story about how individuals enter into group coaching, what they experience while they're there, what they achieve as outcomes of their participation, and how those outcomes influence their meaning making with regard to self and entrepreneurship. Both participants in the pilot study entered into group coaching at specific inflection points in their lives and businesses. Prompted by a search for direction and a clear path forward, these business owners found group coaching to be a fertile learning environment. The particular characteristics of group coaching environments, coupled with the coaches' roles as group facilitators and purveyors of knowledge, set the stage for meaningful peer learning on multiple levels.

Outcomes from participation ranged from the acquisition and application of practical business knowledge, to increases in self-awareness and personal understanding consistent with higher-level learning. More importantly, the data showed an evolving discourse on entrepreneurship characterized by the deconstruction of old assumptions about business and success and the acquisition of new discursive resources. Participants drew from these resources in their groups and in the interviews to construct new personal theories of entrepreneurship and emergent notions of self-as-entrepreneur.

**Key takeaways from the pilot.** The pilot study demonstrated that my chosen methods were well-suited for my inquiry, and that only minor changes to the study methods were necessary. Additional takeaways included lessons learned about narrative interviewing, and further learning that influenced the design and products of this study. I describe all of these takeaways in detail below.

Minor changes to the study methods included

- Revisions to my Interview Guide (Appendix E) to make it simpler and more practical, to improve its organization, and to make it more useful as a tool for tracking conversations with participants.

- The addition of a Participant Setup Checklist (Appendix C) to help me keep track of all the information I need to convey to participants in advance of their interviews.

The pilot study also provided opportunities to practice narrative interviewing, which allowed me to identify ways of improving my interviewing skills as I engaged in data collection for the main study. Key takeaways included

- Learning to recognize avenues for personal story when I hear them.

- Learning to ask simpler questions.

- Learning to listen on multiple levels (e.g., for personal story, for discursive

  resources, and for relational context) to what is occurring in the interviews.

On a deeper level, the process of collecting and analyzing data led to rich learning that further influenced my thinking about the design and products of the study. Specifically, the pilot study influenced my thinking about (a) my participants' life stories, (b) how I would present those stories in the final report, and (c) incorporating thematic methods. I discuss each of these below.

*Participants' life stories.* I was surprised by the extent to which my participants described some of the historical aspects of their lives (family, education, upbringing, life paths, etc.) that have influenced their assumptions about entrepreneurship. I had expected to hear stories bound within concrete experiences of group coaching, but instead gained a sense of the broader life trajectories of both participants, and of how their group coaching experiences intersected with those trajectories. I began to think more about eliciting life stories (versus bounded events in a group coaching context) as a result. Turning the study in this direction allowed for a deeper exploration of participants' identity work and discursive constructions as entrepreneurs, and of the role group coaching has played in influencing/supporting/challenging/developing those constructions.

*Presentation of stories.* Given the nature of the life stories that my participants told, I found it important to think carefully about how the higher-order stories constructed from my narrative analysis should be presented in the final report. This led to my choice to present the stories as longer-form narratives, rather than as smaller fragments that might be used to support a thematic presentation of the findings. Casting participants' narratives in a more holistic and detailed form allowed me to deeply explore the differences between them. It also helped to place participants' group coaching experiences within the broader context of their long-held assumptions about entrepreneurship and entrepreneurial identity.

*Incorporating thematic methods.* Presenting only long-form narratives as findings would've limited the study by failing to explore the meaning of the entire collection of stories taken together. The stories themselves may be interesting and informative; but taken as a whole, what do they convey about the meaning entrepreneurs make of their experiences in group coaching? This question called for the addition of a thematic component to analysis. As discussed above, I have therefore included both narrative and thematic analytical methods in the main study, and this is reflected in the way my findings are organized and presented in Chapter 4.

## Summary

In this chapter I have described in detail my proposed research approach and design; including methods of data collection and analysis, sampling strategy, validity, researcher reflexivity, and preliminary findings and takeaways from the pilot study. I have argued that a narrative-qualitative approach is appropriate for exploring the research phenomenon under investigation in this study. I have also documented some of the fundamental challenges and tensions in narrative research, and have explored the ways in which those tensions intersect with the study. Finally, I have positioned myself as a researcher by attending to several issues of reflexivity and anticipating their influence on the research project.

## CHAPTER FOUR: FINDINGS

This study explored the experience of group coaching as a setting for individual

learning and change in entrepreneurs. The research question was, *Given the impact of social*

*processes on entrepreneurial learning and identity, what does it mean to entrepreneurs to*

*navigate their learning-related challenges in the context of a coaching group?* In this

chapter I present the findings from the study.

The study revealed three different types or categories of phenomena that participants

either directly associated with their meaningful group coaching experiences, or that they

illustrated through their storied accounts. The first are the *background conditions or*

*characteristics* that participants associated with their coaching groups. The second is *a range*

*of "process moves"* reflected in participants' stories of their defining moments in group

coaching. The third category is comprised of the *discursive moves or actions performed*

*within the relational context of the interview itself* that contributed to participants' meaning-

making processes. These discursive moves can be thought of as elements of the unfolding

conversation between interviewer and participant that directly influenced participants'

constructions of past events and their meaning. This chapter is organized into three parts,

each reflecting one of these three types of phenomena.

In Part 1, I discuss the background conditions described in connection with

participants' meaningful experiences in group coaching. These include characteristics of the

social environment, characteristics of the social processes at work in the group, and

characteristics of the coach's presence in the group. In Part 2, I present a collection of

vignettes illustrating a range of process moves (processes of learning and change) that unfold

over time and through specific sequences of events in group coaching. The data revealed two broad categories of process moves: moves that reflect *learning vicariously* and moves that reflect *learning through feedback.*

Finally, in Part 3 I present a series of vignettes which illustrate the impact of the relational context of the interview itself on participants' retrospective constructions of their meaningful group coaching experiences. I explore three types of exchanges between participant and interviewer that influenced participants' constructions of their past events: *negotiating belonging, co-creating successful entrepreneurship,* and *co-creating conscious learning.* These "discursive performances" highlight the co-constructed nature of narrative data and the influence of the researcher on participants' meaning making and learning. My interpretations and discussion are presented in Chapter 5.

The three sections also reflect the influence of different analytical paths taken in this research. As described above, I used both narrative and thematic methods to analyze my data, and these different methods led to different types of findings. Part 1, for example, draws primarily from a thematic mode of analysis, where participants' descriptions of the coaching environment are taken at face value and categorical groupings stretch across the data. Results from narrative analysis on the other hand help locate participants' stories in their historical and relational contexts. They emphasize individual meaning making and include information about the narrator's intention and the researcher's influence on the production of the data. The results in Part 3 reflect these narrative principles. Viewed as a continuum, the process moves described in Part 2 sit in between these influences and draw from both narrative and thematic methods. They represent higher-order themes that stretch across the data set, but they also illustrate distinct temporal sequences and explore that narrator's use of language.

## Part 1: Conditions

Common conditions or characteristics of the coaching group and its activities form a backdrop for group members' meaningful experiences. The background conditions that participants described in connection with their meaningful group coaching experiences fall broadly into three categories: *characteristics of the social environment of the group*, *characteristics of the social processes at work in the group*, and *characteristics of the coach's presence in the group*. These conditions are reflected in the ways that participants talked about their coaching groups and what happens in them. I discuss each of these categories in detail below.

### Social Environment

Meaningful experiences in group coaching rest importantly on the other people in the room. The first category of background conditions that participants described in connection with their meaningful group coaching experiences includes characteristics of the social environment of the group. The stories that participants told bring to light two interrelated aspects of the group social environment: *cohesiveness* and *commonality*. Group cohesiveness, as defined by Yalom and Leszcz (2005), refers to the "groupness" or "attractiveness of a group for its members" (pp. 54-55). I use the term here to represent the spirit of belonging and togetherness that participants described through their stories about their coaching groups. I use the term "commonality" here to refer to the sense that one's experience is shared and/or deeply understood by others; in other words, the sense that one is not alone in her/his experience.

**Cohesiveness.** Entrepreneurs form close relationships with their peers in the group. Where cohesiveness is concerned, most participants described their groups in terms of the warm and caring relationships they developed with other group members, their fondness for the group itself, and their sense of belonging. Several participants described their peers in the group as friends or close friends despite never having met before joining their groups. Rigsby, for example, spoke about having a camaraderie with her peers in the group, while Lynn described the other members of her group as "very good friends."

Here, Belinda talks about her friendships with group members and her relationship to the group itself:

> I didn't know the other members of the group at first. But, um, no, now—now we're like a really close-knit group.

> I feel like these are friends now that, like, you know, occasionally they'll check in and just be like, "Hey, just—you know, you had—you were having surgery this week, how're you feeling?" and that sort of stuff.

> I mean, it's a group of people that I think you develop relationships with that are looking out for you personally and for your business.

> I mean, I really—I have a hard time imagining not having the group.

Belinda's comments indicate that her relationships with group members extend outside of their monthly sessions, and that she views her group as something more than a place she visits once a month to learn about business. It has become an enduring resource for friendship and caring relationships in her life, both business and personal in nature. Her words, "I have a hard time imagining not having the group" illustrate the close-knit nature of these relationships and the importance she places on her membership in the group.

The notion of belonging is echoed by Ted, despite his initial reluctance about joining the group:

> [Julie] strong-armed me into it. [laughs]  She did.
>
> …because, I hate to say this, but it's like, I never saw myself as needing a business coach.  It's like I know what I know, I'm right, I don't need somebody telling me what to do.  That's why I left corporate America.  And—and I think part of it is some of the answers to questions that I might have, I already know the answers to, but they're answers I don't want to know, I don't want to hear, and I don't want to be held accountable.  That's it. [laughs] I'm admitting it.
>
> …and that's why I really wasn't thrilled with it.
>
> And, um, [Julie] invited me back.  I still didn't wanna go. [laughs]  I did see value, but I didn't wanna go back.  But as I got to know these folks, it, um, it's become my little group now.  So they're not just people that are there, they've become acquaintances.  Or—or colleagues.
>
> It just—you know, the longer I would go and we would have interaction, it became comfortable.  And when I became comfortable then, yeah, this is—this is our group, you know?  I belong, we belong, you know, all that.

Ted's comments suggest that the value he derives from group coaching comes more from having found a group of peers he feels comfortable with than from the kind of accountability-driven coaching approach he expected.  The experience of belonging that develops over time allows him to overcome his own reluctance and skepticism.  As these comments illustrate, participants found the cohesiveness of their groups to be an important aspect of their meaningful group coaching experiences.

**Commonality.**  Meaningful bonds between group members emerge through shared experience.  Several participants made reference to feeling as though others in the group understood and could relate to their entrepreneurial experiences.  In particular, they noted feeling that their peers share similar goals and challenges, feeling a "common bond" with their peers in the group, and feeling as though they are not alone.  Eleanor, for example, talked about struggling in other business-related group situations and finding her coaching group to be a very different type of experience.

> That—that was tough for me to get used to.  I am very introverted and, um, that's why
> I like working alone.
>
> Uh, so getting out there in a group, like in person, like networking, that's very
> difficult for me.  And in fact, it, you know, two years ago I just totally gave up
> networking.  I just didn't wanna deal with it anymore.
>
> But the, uh, but the group coaching, because we were in similar situations and had
> likeminded goals and objectives for ourselves and we're experiencing the same kinds
> of challenges, obstacles, that didn't feel like it was a networking group.  It didn't feel
> like I was out there selling myself.  It felt like I was there to support someone who
> was going through something and giving the expertise that I had and the experience
> that I learned, and I was getting that in return.

Eleanor's comments indicate that the similar situations, goals, and challenges experienced by members of the coaching group helped her view this group as an opportunity to support others and learn from their expertise, instead of to sell.  Her words paint a stark contrast between how she experiences her group (supporting and supportive) and how she experiences other types of networking groups ("out there," selling herself, etc.).  Rigsby described a similar sense of commonality in her group, noting that although different group members have different businesses, they face common challenges:

> And it's just been cool to see different people come in and out and, um, different
> businesses but always similar challenges.  Um, and you usually find, you know,
> depending on the size of the group, there's usually someone in the group that's totally
> going through what you're going through or that just dealt with it.

While Eleanor and Rigsby spoke mostly of commonality in terms of the circumstances of their businesses (i.e., situations, goals, challenges, etc.), Pierre spoke about how sharing vulnerability with other group members ultimately made him feel less alone.  In the excerpts below, he tells the story of his initial doubts about the group, his surprise at hearing common themes in other group members' stories, and the impact of developing this common bond.

I was reluctant. I was really reluctant. And, umm, I just kind of jumped in anyway. And I thought, "Okay, if this is a disaster after the first couple meetings, umm, then, you know, I'll bow out, but I'll at least try. I'll give it a chance."

I had pre-judged it in my own mind that I was gonna get much more out of a one-on-one with a coach than I was out of a group. Umm, and, uhh, and so I ended up being mistaken about that. Umm, and, uhh, so I—I had some prejudice, definitely, going in.

Pierre's initial prejudice against the group environment bears similarity to Eleanor's experience, but they are alike for different reasons. Eleanor's reluctance stemmed from her introversion and the pressure she felt in business networking groups to get "out there" and sell herself. Pierre admitted that his reluctance stemmed from his concern that being in a group meant less time devoted to his own challenges, and hence less value overall. He explains below how his view shifted.

…what I found very early on, umm, was that, uhh, basically you're—you're involving yourself in a partnership, and—and so, umm, there's a sense of community when you start sharing your—your story with other people, and I was super surprised at all the common themes.

I really shifted gears into, umm, not coming from the perspective so much of, "What am I going to get out of this? How much can I get out in the shortest amount of time?" which is why I was thinking, you know, one-on-one was better, umm, but embracing the fact that, uhh, you're in an environment where the whole point is to share your vulnerabilities.

By doing that and being as honest as I could about, umm, things that I didn't feel good about or shortcomings or any of that, umm, and everybody else trying to do that as well, umm, you sort of—you start to get a bond going and it's just—it's a sense of community where you feel like, "Oh, I—I used to think all my inadequacies were mine on my own little desert island, and now I realize that, no, these are things that, like, everybody's facing and, umm, you know, you're not—you're not alone in this."

Umm, so that was—that was kind of the bond between all of us. Even though we'd be sharing different problems, umm, you know, you—you felt like you weren't alone in—in your situation and you shouldn't be as embarrassed as you are about not knowing what to do with that.

Pierre's use of concepts like shortcomings, inadequacy, and embarrassment give added meaning to the experience of commonality and its importance as a background condition of the group coaching environment. Knowing that others shared similar feelings helped challenge a deeply held assumption he held about himself—that his perceived shortcomings separate him from other entrepreneurs. The knowledge that others face similar challenges helped reduce his embarrassment and strengthen his sense of belonging.

According to some participants, another related aspect of their coaching groups had to do with how difficult it can be to find people outside of their group who can understand and relate to what it's like to be an entrepreneur. Lynn, for instance, spoke about how her priorities and her relationship to her work separate her from friends.

> Well, it's hard to sit down with a group of people, just friends or whatever, and talk about what it's like to be an entrepreneur when they work for somebody else because they don't have the risk. In most cases they don't have the commitment. Um, it's not a priority. Work is not a priority. Work is something that they do to pay the bills. Um, in many cases they don't enjoy it. Um, we truly enjoy what we do.

Rigsby mirrors Lynn's thoughts below, adding that although her friends and family are supportive, her ownership of her business makes her situation different.

> I mean, my family and friends were supportive, but, yeah, I don't think—I don't they— they don't—they still don't really understand. Like I'll talk—my mom's a manager at a hospital and I'll talk to her about things, but there's—it's still different when you own it, you know? It's—yeah. So it's hard to relate to people that aren't—you know how that is, like, that aren't in the same situation.

The comments above illustrate the value of finding a sense of commonality with other entrepreneurs who can understand and relate. Participants in this study associated knowing that their peers share similar goals and challenges, feeling a common bond, and feeling as though they are not alone, with their meaningful experiences in group coaching. Group cohesiveness and the experience of commonality were the two most often-noted background conditions related to the group social environment. In the section below, I discuss another category of background conditions: the social processes that participants described in connection with their meaningful group coaching experiences.

**Social Processes**

Meaningful experiences in group coaching arise out of specific types of social interaction between group members. This second category of background conditions that participants described in connection with their meaningful group coaching experiences includes characteristics of the social processes at work in the group. Throughout the interviews, participants frequently described or made reference to three types of social processes at work in their coaching groups: *social support*, *exchange*, and *accountability*. In the context of their stories, social support refers to acts of personal and/or emotional support and encouragement. Some participants talked about receiving this type of support, while others talked about providing it. The term *exchange* is defined by Thornton (2010) as "an encounter with new information." Its use here encompasses the interchange of ideas, information, and feedback between group members. *Accountability* refers to a process whereby group members hold one another to their word for the actions and/or goals they commit to.

**Social support.** Entrepreneurs benefit greatly from receiving emotional support and encouragement from their peers. Overwhelmingly, participants described their coaching groups not only as a source of business knowledge and expertise, but also as a source of personal and/or emotional support and encouragement. They spoke of this type of support as a meaningful and potent aspect of their group experiences—whether they were giving or receiving it, and regardless of whether the focus of the support was business-related or personal in nature.  This aspect of the groups prompted some comparisons to therapy, as

Eleanor commented below.

> It was—some of those sessions were a little like therapy, you know?  Um, it was
> someone saying, you know, "You really—look, you've had this—you know, you've
> done this for, you know, this many years, um, you have this many clients, you know,
> you have, um, a great support network back in California.  What makes you think
> that, you know, people here [in Arizona] aren't going to recognize the same things?"
> So it was a lot of that just emotional-type support and encouragement.

Eleanor had moved from California to Arizona and was struggling to establish herself in her

new locale when she joined her coaching group.  The group's encouragement, coupled with

advice she received from group members, helped boost her confidence and enabled her to

start networking and building support for her business.

Rigsby and Belinda describe their groups in similar terms below, emphasizing the

fact that the support given to group members extends into the context of their personal lives.

Rigsby spoke about supporting another group member whose entrepreneurial path was

adversely affecting his family.

> Personal stuff comes into it too.  Like, um, one of the other people in our group, um,
> his spouse, you know, has a lot of issues with his entrepreneurial side, you know, so
> things like that where it's like—it's more than just your business, it's like, "Business is
> affecting my family, my spouse.  You know, how am I gonna deal with this?"  And so
> sometimes it turns into more like therapy in a way because it's like, "Well, have you
> considered this?  You know, maybe she's feeling this way," or—or whatever.

Belinda described how her group supported her during a recent bout with several health

issues, noting that it makes a difference for her just to know there is a group of people who

care about her.

> I just ran into this, like, really bad cycle of health issues and, like, it just kept getting
> worse and worse and worse and, like, you know, I was incredibly depressed and, um,
> I've since had two out of three surgeries that are gonna be, like, associated with all of
> this timeframe.

But, you know, like, meeting with the group once a month, like, it was, you know, it wasn't really even asking me about my business. And, you know, like, they would and they'd ask, you know, "What have you got going on?" and "Is there anything we can help you with?" but it was more, "What's going on? What's—what's next? What have you learned from those tests?" Like, you know, so it was just—it kind of almost was more like group therapy at times.

The group has been very supportive and—and it's just nice to have that outlet, uh, and, you know, it gives you a place to unload some of your baggage but also, like, to reload some support and, you know, know that there are people out there that care.

I was surprised by how centrally the role of social support factored into some participants' conceptualizations of their groups' activities. Scott, for example told a story about supporting a woman in his group who was going through a difficult time. In this particular session the group bypassed its planned agenda and focused on letting the woman talk though her circumstances. Scott explained that he likes that fact that his group prioritizes its group members' most pressing needs above any planned agenda.

There was one woman who was going through very, very tough things at home and in work. And she had one night where, I mean, all of us in the group just let her kind of bounce her thoughts off us and we just—the whole group focused on her issues and her things and tried to boost her and tried to help her. It was a really, I mean, that was a great session.

So, I mean, so that's the thing. It's—the thing I like about the coaching is it doesn't have to be, you know, we always sort of have a lesson plan and we always sort of touch base with each other on successes and challenges, but if somebody's really got an issue and they need help, the coach sort of goes, "Okay, we'll put that aside and let's—let's help you out." And I like that.

Finally, for participants in this study, social support also encompasses encouraging and validating group members' ideas and choices. Lynn, for example, reflected on how her group encouraged and supported her when she decided to start her tech business.

So I took it to my group and I said, "I think I'm gonna try this. I don't know how, I don't—I can't develop software, I need resources, I've never done this before. This is completely out of my element. I know how to market it, but I don't really know the foundations of building it. And I've got the go-ahead at home."

> They were like, "That is awesome.  Totally think you should do that.  That would be great."  So supportive.

In addition to her description of the group's response to her idea, Lynn's use of language in this section underlines something about the process of social support that she finds meaningful.  Her words, "So I took it to my group," convey a sense of easiness and familiarity.  Taking it to her group, as opposed to "presenting it" or "proposing it" (for example) shows that this process is both familiar and informal—something she does on a regular basis.  It is something she feels confident (if not comfortable) doing.  In this context, the process of social support began for Lynn with her way of relating to the group—as a resource for support, rather than as an evaluative, critical, or competitive audience.

In summary, participants in this study described their coaching groups as a source of personal and/or emotional support and encouragement, and told stories of both supporting their peers and being supported.  The focus of social support can be personal, business-related, or both—as in Rigsby's case.  Furthermore, the processes of helping and supporting group members can sometimes bypass or derail the group's planned agenda, and this is both expected and appreciated.  The groups are seen by their members as a resource for support and encouragement (sometimes resembling therapy), and the paths by which members access this support are familiar and informal.  In the next section, I explore participants' descriptions of another social process at work in their groups—*exchange*—which encompasses the interchange of ideas, information, and feedback between group members.

**Exchange.**  A vibrant interchange of ideas, information, and feedback functions as an engine of learning and change for group members.  Several participants described or told stories about meaningful interactions of this nature.  These encounters with new information (Thornton, 2010) were seen as a central component of the groups' regular and ongoing activities. Participants noted the reciprocal nature of exchange in their groups (receiving and giving), and the fact that it can occur either during or outside of group coaching sessions.

The exchange of ideas came up frequently in my interviews. Rigsby recalled having an opportunity to shadow a more experienced peer in her group outside of their monthly group coaching session. After sitting in on some of his meetings and then debriefing together, he gave her ideas for how to incorporate learning and development into her staff's day-to-day work.

In another example, Eleanor talked about getting an idea to create a guidebook on employee turnover to help clients of her HR consultancy cope with their staffing challenges. The idea came from another group member who had created a guidebook for parents of troubled children who were clients of her therapy practice. Ted talked about receiving an idea from another group member to send handwritten postcards to potential clients as a way of building business relationships and differentiating himself from competitors.

In addition to exchanging concrete ideas for generating business and managing relationships with customers and staff, several participants described exchanging information and advice with other group members. For example, Eleanor spoke about learning from other group members how to use social media to market her business after her move to Arizona. Having access to this information through her coaching group ended up saving her time and energy in ways she never expected.

> Um, so I was open to, uh, more social media interaction or using social media to market the business more. And, um, some of the women in the group had those experiences already. They had been active in social media or they had created networking groups in their own communities.

> So having those different... perspectives also from women who had already set up, um, you know, shopping carts on their website and were very active on LinkedIn and, um, could tell me, "Oh, get—go—sign up for Hootsuite because that's gonna help

you. You know, you can load all your social media in there for the week and time it to go out so you're not sitting there every day posting something." Well, I had no clue about that. So, wow, did that save me time and energy, you know?

Some of the participants specifically emphasized the reciprocal nature of exchange in their groups. In other words, exchange can also be about contributing ideas, information, and advice to others. Ted shared with me that when other group members talk about their challenges, he listens to see if he can add or interject anything from his own experience that may be helpful. Lynn indicated that she values the opportunity to provide input into other people's challenges.

> I also loved giving input. Who doesn't like to give their opinion? I love to give my opinion! [laughs] Just give me an invitation! So, you know, we'd sit around the table and they'd be like, "Oh, I'm really struggling, I'm trying to do this," and you're—it's an opportunity to motivate people, it's an opportunity to have input into a different area of life that maybe you've never dabbled in before.

> For me, I just—I love it because I'm like, "Well, have you ever thought about doing this?" "Hmm." Or, "Yes, I did. I tried that and it didn't work." "Okay, well, you know." We all have so much knowledge and why not swap it? [laughs] Share with one another.

Both she and Eleanor mentioned that it was important to them to help others avoid the kinds of difficulties that they had faced along the way. In the excerpt below, Lynn notes how helping others avoid some of the mistakes she made herself can be very rewarding.

> I may feel unfulfilled at a particular time in my life and I may be very confused about it, but being able to help somebody else is still gonna give me a satisfaction of knowing that, like, you know, well, you know, at least—my—my whole thing my whole life has been through—I've made some really bad choices and done some bad things, but when it comes down to it, if I can take the knowledge away from it and give that to somebody else to help them to maybe not go through the same thing, I would love it. And we all know that our children aren't gonna listen to us, so I might as well give that knowledge to somebody who actually wants it.

Finally, the processes involved in exchange include giving and receiving feedback to and from other group members. This feedback can be either affirming or challenging in nature. Feedback can function as a sounding board for group members' ideas and/or as a mirror for their behaviors and choices. In addition, group feedback sometimes functions as an interruption or a challenge to modes of thinking and/or action that group members consider to be unproductive or ineffective.

Lynn used her group as a sounding board when she presented her idea for her tech business (see above). She was able to receive feedback on her plan before making the final decision to start Tagsale.com. Scott had started hiring contract employees over the past year and received feedback from his group that helped him create policies and procedures for hiring. Rigsby received feedback from a group member about what motivates her and how she approaches her work (I present a detailed account of this experience and what she learned from it in Part 2 below).

Perhaps more surprising is the role that interrupting or challenging feedback played in several of the participants' stories. For example, Pierre received feedback from group members that challenged his long-held assumptions about his abilities as a writer (this story is also told in detail in Part 2 below). Lynn remarked that her group members will "point out, like, when you're crazy, you know? Which is actually pretty good." Rigsby recalled an incident below that pushed her to challenge a group member's relationship with a business partner.

> One woman just joined our group and she has a partner, a business partner. And they're already having issues, like, three months into their partnership.

> And, you know, it's the kind of place where you can say, "This is alarming. Like, this might be an indicator that you need to cut ties with this woman and do this."

> And I expect the same from them. And you need that. I mean, sometimes you just need somebody to call you out and, um—and maybe they haven't thought of it, but if someone else is pointing it out and it's that obvious that someone else can point it out, well, maybe that's something I need to think about. You know?

Feedback that challenges or interrupts, according to stories like these, is given from the same background of caring and support from which affirming feedback is given. The difference is that challenging feedback is given out of concern when a group member appears to be veering down an unproductive path or viewing a situation from a limited perspective. When asked what distinguishes the feedback provided in group coaching as opposed to other business community groups or activities, Scott replied, "I think it creates a setting where people can challenge you. You know… if you're heading in directions or making statements that, um, people with maybe more experience than you know aren't valid, they'll challenge you. And that's great."

To summarize before moving on, participants in this study highlighted the exchange of ideas, information, and feedback as important social processes at work in their groups. Their stories revealed that exchange encompasses concrete business ideas, but also information and advice aimed at specific situations or challenges, and feedback that either affirms or challenges a group member's thinking and actions. The reciprocal nature of exchange was also important to some group members as it allowed them to contribute in ways that presumably helped others avoid mistakes they had made themselves. Having explored the phenomena of social support and exchange above, I explore social processes related to accountability in the next section below.

**Accountability.** Entrepreneurs crave accountability and find this through group coaching. Accountability refers to a process whereby group members hold one another to their word for the actions and/or goals they commit to. Participants repeatedly mentioned accountability as an important function of their groups and a useful source of motivation.

Below, Scott talks about the structures his group uses to set and manage group members'

goals and commitments.

> One of the things with—with our coaching group is every time we meet there—there
> are forms we get that challenge us to reflect on things or to do homework for the next
> time to think about how we're growing our business, um, you know, definite—
> definite steps.  Quarterly we look at where are we at quarterly, what have we
> accomplished, are we taking steps to truly, like, grow.  Um, and the group holds you
> accountable to that.

He goes on to explain how this structure of accountability helps him step outside of the day-

to-day work of his business and pay attention to the bigger picture.

> I think my biggest struggle is I have a tendency to quickly fall into the, "I've just gotta
> do my job." I'm not thinking about, "I'm a business.  Am I keeping—looking at the
> big picture too?" So for me, having people kind of go, "Well, what did you do this
> month to, you know, think about your business?"

When speaking about being asked about his actions, Scott's choice of the word "people"

implies a collective understanding of how accountability functions in the group.  In other

words, it is understood to be something the group holds collectively for its members, rather

than a conversation imposed solely by the coach or another individual.  Other participants'

stories corroborate this understanding.

According to Belinda, the idea of having a group of people to help hold her

accountable was part of what motivated her to join her group.

> We talk about our goals and we have people that are there to help hold us accountable
> to them, and I was like, "That's probably not a bad idea for me," because I can—I can
> be a little squirrel chaser sometimes and it's—for somebody to be like, "Hey, [snaps
> fingers] hello!" [laughs]

She also spoke about how accountability is woven into her group's activities and

expectations about behavior.  Here she talks about another group member who veered away

from her stated goals:

> And then the next month she was buying a house and, like, suddenly, like, all of these things that, like—in terms of the accountability group, you know, you set these goals and, like, you talk about where you are in your life and what's going on and, like, all of a sudden she's buying houses and we're like, "What? That wasn't on her goal sheet. What is she doing?"

This example suggests that the social expectation of accountability affects the way group members relate to each other's actions and behaviors. The data also show how Belinda responds to this expectation herself by taking action she wouldn't otherwise take:

> Like I feel like it helps, having these other people that are watching me and paying attention to whether or not I'm reaching my goals. And so how does that make me look if I'm not reaching them? So how—how… [are my peers] going to talk about me if I'm not getting somewhere towards my goals? You know, if they—if they keep seeing me being lazy or failing or whatever the case may be, how is that fair? So—or how is that—how is that going to make it look to them?

> Like I can't imagine not being part of the group because it makes—it motivates me just a little bit. If it's just this much, I need it.

Her comments reveal the social pressure or group-level dissonance generated by the expectation of accountability. Belinda's concern about how she will look or how the group will view her if she fails to make progress toward her goals is a significant motivator for her. At the same time, these data show a connection in Belinda's mind between the way she wants to be known by her group (her identity) and her ability to follow through on her commitments.

Another illustration of this process came from Eleanor, who described some of the actions she committed to and alluded to the same social pressure to keep her commitment:

> …and then it was, uh, "Report back to the next meeting"—you know, we made a commitment at the end of each meeting that we were going to accomplish something, um, before the next meeting that we had on the phone. So some of my assignments were to attend, you know, X number of networking meetings, to make, uh, uh, you know, maybe two or three coffee dates with individuals that I would like to get to know better or that were in my target market, that kind of thing. So, um, having that accountability to the women in the group was very helpful because I didn't wanna disappoint them.

Eleanor states that her motivation comes at least partly from not wanting to disappoint her peers. She doesn't explicitly connect the risk of disappointing others with the maintenance of her identity in the group, as Belinda did. However, the fact that she mentions not wanting to disappoint them implies that she views keeping her word as a way of negotiating her identity claims.

In contrast to all of these accounts, Mila indicated that the social structure of accountability provided by her group was not meaningful or valuable to her at this stage of her development as an entrepreneur. She stressed the importance of finding the right fit in a group, and talked about why this aspect of her group wasn't working well for her.

> M: I like group settings, I have no problem with that, but it's finding the right group setting. That's the biggest thing.
>
> With the one what I'm doing with Julie… where are you at with your goals? Not doing it for me anymore. If you're a little bit more advanced, you gotta find a group that's gonna advance you even further. I don't need to go back and do goals every week, goals every week and meet once a month.
>
> In the beginning I needed that to—to say, um, uh, checks and boundaries, you know, am I doing this? Somebody who could make sure that I'm doing it. But now I think I'm a little bit past that, that I can do that for myself to figure out what I'm doing and stuff. So for me now it's knowledge as far as figuring out where I wanna take the business. I need to learn more about, um, what'd I just tell them? That damn cash flow.

Even though Mila was the only participant who expressed these feelings about accountability and goal setting, the idea of finding a group that offers the right fit was echoed by Scott. For Mila, fit is about offering the right type of support at the right stage of personal development. For Scott, fit is about partnering with other entrepreneurs who share his level of commitment and experience.

To summarize, accountability refers to a process whereby group members hold one another to their word for the actions and/or goals they commit to. This phenomenon turned up in the majority of interviews as an important function of the coaching groups and as a useful source of motivation. According to the participants in this study, the social expectation of accountability is held collectively by their groups and carries implications not only for action, but for identity negotiation as well. In the next section I will explore the third broad category of background conditions: those that relate to the coach's presence in the group.

**The Coach's Presence**

Meaningful experiences in group coaching are shaped and influenced by what coaches bring to the table. The third category of conditions that participants associated with their meaningful group coaching experiences includes characteristics of the coach's presence in the group. Given the similarities apparent in their descriptions of their coaching groups above, one might assume that the coaches themselves influenced the groups in mostly similar (if not identical) ways. Surprisingly, this was not the case. Participants described the role and influence of each of the three coaches in distinct ways. According to these descriptions, each coach contributed their own emphasis or approach to their group(s). Broadly speaking, the various emphases were *applying cognitive models or frameworks* (Naomi), *asking the right questions* (Susan), and *managing accountability* (Julie).

In Naomi's case, Pierre described two different cognitive frameworks that Naomi used as lenses for coaching activities and discussions in his group. One was called the "New Money Story." Naomi used it to help Pierre and his peers surface and examine their unconscious beliefs about money and self-worth. The second, called "the saboteur assessment," involved identifying different internal voices that occupy the roles of sage and

saboteur. Pierre referred to working with both of these models as important and meaningful

components of his group coaching experience. None of the other participants in this study

mentioned any specific cognitive models or frameworks used by their coaches.

When Eleanor spoke about Susan's role as a coach, she focused on Susan's ability to

ask the right questions "to keep the discussion going and guide us in a way that we came to

our own conclusions." She likened this role to that of a flagger on the airport tarmac.

> She was there to give us a lot of, um, I don't know, maybe like when the, um,
> airplane is, um, trying to taxi into the, you know, into the gate and the guys are out
> there waving their directional, you know, they're not flags, they're those little, like,
> flashlight kinds of things. And they're guiding—the pilot knows exactly where to go,
> right? He knows or she knows where the gate is, but here's this person giving them,
> "A little more to the left," you know, "Forward, forward," that kind of thing. So I—
> that, I think, was Susan's, um, uh, big contribution to this whole process.

Eleanor also recalled how Susan's precise questioning helped her learn vicariously from

another group member. This story is told in detail in the next section.

Participants in Julie's groups, on the other hand, focused on her ability to manage

accountability with each group member. This involved following up on each group

member's goals and commitments, directing them toward actionable steps, holding them to

account, and so on.

> Rigsby: She's always checking in with us, you know, "How's it going on your 30-day
> goal or—or your overall goal?" And she, like I said, she's not—her big plus is that
> she's not afraid to call you out on stuff.

> Belinda: So, you know… she recognizes that sometimes our coaching sessions are
> going to be Belinda meltdowns because of X, Y, and Z. And so, like, sometimes she
> just plays the role of therapist during our coaching sessions. And then it's, "Okay, so
> we got that off our chest. Now what goals do you have for this month? And let's
> write them down so that way you at least have them and move forward," and then
> she'll check in on me, you know, like, just make sure that I haven't fallen off the face
> of the planet.

> Lynn: Helping you keep your priorities lined out to where you don't lose yourself in the mix or forget about the things that you really wanna do. You know, she's like, "Well, how are you gonna do this and still, you know, hang out with your kids this summer?" Or, you know, whatever it happens to be.

In each of these examples, Julie provides a structure of accountability to hold group members to their commitments, direct them toward future actions, and so on.

It is very likely that each of the coaches draws from other categories at different times, and in a few cases the data support this notion. For instance, Eleanor also described how Susan would direct the group to commit to actions they would take in between sessions, and Pierre mentioned that Naomi was not afraid to hold people to account and often did. A comprehensive exploration of how and what coaches generally contribute to their groups is beyond the scope of this study. What is relevant to this study, however, is that in their descriptions the participants gravitated toward certain features of the coach's contribution to the group, and that these features differed from coach to coach. This despite many similarities across the groups themselves with regard to characteristics of the social environment and social processes discussed above.

In summary, participants described the role and influence of each of the three coaches in distinct ways, broadly influencing the group through applying cognitive models or frameworks (Naomi), asking the right questions (Susan), and managing accountability (Julie). These differences are surprising given the similar ways in which participants described conditions related to the social environments and social processes of their groups. However, it is also important to note that participants' comments about how their coaches approached their groups should not be taken as an accurate or complete representation of the coaches' methods. They are, rather, reflections of what participants spoke about most in connection with the influence of each coach. In addition, it is likely that all three coaches borrow from all three categories at different times and in response to different situations that

arise in their groups.  Further research is needed to better understand how and when coaches

draw from different approaches or methodologies in their practice with groups.

**Conclusion of Part 1**

As discussed above, the background conditions that participants described in

connection with their meaningful group coaching experiences fall broadly into three

categories: characteristics of the social environment of the group, characteristics of the social

processes at work in the group, and characteristics of the coach's presence in the group.

These conditions are reflected in the ways that participants talked about their coaching

groups and what happens in them.

The participants characterized the social environment of their groups in terms of

cohesiveness and commonality.  Cohesiveness represents their warm and caring relationships

with other group members, their fondness for the group itself, and their sense of belonging.

Commonality refers to feeling that their peers share similar goals and challenges, feeling a

common bond with their peers in the group, and feeling as though they are not alone.

The study identified three types of social processes at work in the groups:  social

support, exchange, and accountability.  Social support encompasses the idea that the group

can be a source of personal and/or emotional support and encouragement for members.

Exchange refers to the interchange of ideas, information, and feedback—both general and

specific in nature.  Accountability refers to a process whereby group members hold one

another to their word for the actions and/or goals they commit to.  Finally, participants

described the role and influence of each of the three coaches in distinct ways, broadly

influencing the group through applying cognitive models or frameworks (Naomi), asking the right questions (Susan), and managing accountability (Julie). In Part 2 (of three) below, I discuss a range of possible process moves illustrated by participants' stories of their defining moments in group coaching.

## Part 2: Process Moves

Against the background conditions discussed above, group members engage in dynamic and impactful processes of learning and change. The study revealed a range of possible process moves illustrated by participants' stories of their meaningful or defining moments in group coaching. The moves reflect individual and social processes of learning and change that unfold over time and through specific sequences of events. Two broad types or categories of moves emerged from the data: moves that demonstrate *learning vicariously* and moves that demonstrate *learning through feedback*. In Part 2 below, I present a series of short vignettes illustrating moves from each of these categories. For each category I provide a detailed analysis of the process moves and their impact on the participants' lives and businesses. Before concluding, I explore the counter narratives of two participants who do not describe their group coaching experiences in terms that reflect meaningful learning or change.

### Learning Vicariously

Group members' meaningful experiences in group coaching often involve engaging with and learning from their peers' experiences. The first three vignettes illustrate different process moves demonstrating vicarious learning (learning from the behavior of others) and change. They are participants' stories about being deeply involved in another group member's unfolding experience, learning from that involvement, and applying their learning in specific ways.

In the first, Belinda tells the story of helping another group member go through a transition, and what she learned from being involved. In the second, Scott tells the story of another group member's attempt to start a business and what he learned from it. In the third, Eleanor recalls learning from a business idea another group member implemented. I follow the vignettes with an analysis of the different but related process moves they illustrate.

## Going Through That With Her (Belinda)

In this vignette Belinda talks about helping another group member, Lynn, as Lynn goes through a major transition with Tagsale.com, the business she founded. Belinda, the owner of an interior design business, describes the events, the role the group played in helping Lynn navigate her transition, and what she learned from this experience below.

> B: Lynn… has always been, like, super energetic and ambitious and during—because I've—I've been there long enough that I saw some of this transition as Tagsale.com was really growing, but then as it started to, like, level off and started to shrink, like, Lynn started to really, like, fold up and get really angry and upset about how things were happening and, like, how people were treating her as the owner of the site. Like, I mean, it was just really—like, she was getting a lot of animosity, like, from a lot of different people and it just—it didn't make sense and she was frustrated and it was visible.

> So she started talking about, like, closing down Tagsale.com. And this was her baby and, you know, it had come so far and so part of the—the role of the group was to help her make that decision and—and help her make that transition. And so, like, I— I remember going through that with her where, you know, she finally decided, like, "Okay, I'm going to do this."

> And so we all—those of us who have closed businesses in the past, you know, I'm like, "Okay, well, I had to have my attorney draft letters, um, to all of my clients because I would be surrendering assignments in some cases and, um, you know, so I

had an attorney involved for mine." And so she, you know, talked to people and figured out what she needed to do. And so, like, I just—I remember, like, the group really just helping her through that.

And once it was closed, um, you know, there were a few things that, like, every month we, you know, we'd check in like, "What's left to do to, you know, finally close it out?" and it was, you know, releasing the website, you know, and stop paying for the domain so it's back out there in the world and all that sort of stuff.

And—and, you know, she would talk about, like, "It's really hard for me to just let go of tagsale.com because that's my thing and now it's gonna be out there for somebody else if they wanted it." But so, you know, it was just a process. So I just remember that process for Lynn, that it was everybody contributing what they knew about the process and encouraging her and telling her, you know, that "This—this is the best move for you." And it has been. She's definitely a much happier human being.

In the section below, Belinda talks about what she learned from this experience and

how she applied it in her own business.

B: I don't know what [the "takeaway"] would be off the top of my head, but, um, like, recognizing what's not working and where you need to be spending your time, I think. Um, and since that time, I mean, I have—I mentioned partnering with a real estate company. It's a way for me to keep, I guess, a more steady income going. So that's just kind of like a—a good—and that's honestly how I've managed to bring the business out of the red is to be able to have this home showing aspect of what I do.

E: So, great example. Help me connect that back to Lynn's story.

B: Well, just that you—she was identifying what worked and what didn't work. And so I was—I, you know, I knew that I wasn't making any money with my business and people were hounding me about getting into real estate for a long time and I'm like, "I don't wanna do it, I don't wanna do it." So when this opportunity came up to just be a showing agent instead of a full-fledged real estate agent, like, "Okay, I can do that!" Like I—I can do all of it. So, yeah. So when that opportunity [arose], um, it was, you know, kind of one of those things where it's like, you know, look outside of your box. Um, but yeah, just be able to—to see beyond what you're, like, focusing on and—and see other opportunities outside of it. So I guess that's it.

### This is My Job! (Scott)

In the next vignette, Scott tells the story of how another group member (Rebecca) took some initial steps to launch a business, and how he subsequently challenges her when she is reluctant to continue with the business. Through this sequence of events, Scott learns that he pursues his own business with a completely different mentality.

S: There was a woman who was trying to, in our group, that was trying to take a hobby of hers, which was baking, and she loved to bake desserts and would make all kinds of really, I mean, delicious sweets for people. Um, and Julie was challenging her or giving her opportunities, actually, to expose her business, um, on some events. And, you know, we, um—so we had a situation where she provided stuff for an event and it went, um, I mean, honestly, the event was huge, people loved her stuff, but she was sitting there talking about all the things that went wrong, you know?

E: What was she saying?

S: Oh, it was, um, she got ill, like, the day before because of the stress of it and, um, and she over—you know, she, like, overcooked everything, like, too—made too many of something, you know. And even though it was a success, you know, she had to take some stuff home. And people were asking her about price and she got all stressed out about having to provide a price for her products. And she started back stepping and basically saying, "I don't think I really wanna do this. I don't think I—" you know. I mean, this was, like, her first time actually trying to actually get exposure and instantly she's ready to give up on it. And, you know, she's like, "Well, but I have this job in a… setting where I'm helping as an, you know, administration," and on and on. And I, you know, and I looked at her and I'm like, "You're doing what you love, right?" I'm like, "So why are you even talking like—" I—I just—I got really upset that she was giving up so easily.

S: And, you know, and to me, that was kinda that ah-ha moment for me where I did say, "Look, I don't look at it as, 'I can go to something else,' I go, 'I don't have a plan B or C or D. I'm not—' I'm like, 'This is it. I have to make this successful.'" I go, "I don't—I—I just—I don't even understand someone like you who is saying you wanna do what—your—you love, and yet the first time you have a—a little bit of roughness you're ready to chuck it." I can't—I just—that's so different than my mentality.

So, you know, and I—and I was challenging her. I'm like, "Well then why—why are you even in this group? Because if it's just a social circle, then you're—you, you know, you're in here—I guess that gives you some kind of satisfaction, but that's not helping your business. That's not helping you achieve what you said you loved and wanted to do. This was your passion you were gonna pursue." So, I mean, again, it got pretty confrontational about it. And—and the other people around the group kinda challenged her too, of, you know, "Hey, you just had a success."

E: Wow. So what did you—what did you learn from that whole exchange?

S:  I mean, again, I—it just solidified in my head that—that for me, my business isn't a hobby.  It is truly my passion, it's, um, I guess I just, um, I really don't want it to fail.

## I Really can do This (Eleanor)

In this vignette from Eleanor's interview, she tells the story of how hearing another

group member's idea triggers her to develop a similar idea for her own business.  She talks

about how the whole series of events changed the way she thinks about her business and

herself as an entrepreneur.

El: I guess a way the group worked that was really helpful is, um, one—one of us would talk about, you know, where we are right now, you know, what is it that's been happening that, um, we need some—some help with.  So someone is, say, talking about, um—one was… creating a guidebook, um, for, um, for her clients to deal with their, um, adolescent children.  And so she was developing this guidebook, um, to help with coping mechanisms, um, things to say, um, how to redirect the youngsters, that kind of thing.

Um, well, in that particular session I was able to hear how she was working on developing the guidebook and, uh, kind of a lightbulb went off in my head.  And when she was done speaking and then each of us had a turn to provide feedback, my feedback was, "I can't believe it.  This is exactly what my clients need in terms of working with difficult employees.  And, um, and Tamara, I can see that the steps that you've taken, um, are steps that I could take, with different resources, of course, but steps that I could take to develop a similar sort of set of guidelines, um, you know, to help my, uh, my small business clients."

And one of the problems that my small business clients had and still have is turnover.  And they have, um, you know, it's really hard for them to—to keep good employees for a number of reasons, and, um, I was exploring, you know, what to do about that.  Well, out of that discussion and future discussions in this group I created a small book that, um, I've been selling on, uh, tools to—to handle turnover.  And what that means, how much that costs an employer when turnover keeps happening and happening and what things you need to look at and identify.  And it's not just, um, the wages that are impacted, um, for the business owner, it's the time that's spent, it's the non-productivity, it's the disappointment from the customers because, uh, you know, um,

"There's always somebody new handling my account," that kind of thing.  So based on Tamara's discussion of her handbook for—or guidebook for parents, I got the idea and moved forward in creating this, um, little book on, uh, turnover.

Yeah, yeah, that was the big one because it was after that that I then did really seriously work on the book.  And then, um, from working on the book I worked on a set of tools that, um, we included in the book but then were also available as a standalone on my website.  So it was creating, you know, a couple of different products from one idea.

Er:  Huh.  Wow, that's cool.  That's very cool to see how that develops.  Um, did that—thinking about that experience, uh, did it affect or change the way you saw yourself as an entrepreneur?

El:  Um, I think so.  I think, um, you know, it was like, well, I could—you know, I really can do this.  You know, I—I really can, um, do something other than just, um, coach my own clients, you know, in terms of, um, how they handle employee issues, um, or go in and do some transactional work for them or create their handbook or, um, you know, make responses to the unemployment claims that people are filing.  I could do something that was, um, more foundational, um, something that they could use to really look at their business in a different way and, um, maybe head off some issues that, um, that they—if they had—they acknowledged to see that there were some of these issues in their future, there were ways they could handle them and, um, mitigate the—the pain that, you know, some of that can cause in the business.

**Analysis.**  All three of the vignettes above illustrate processes of learning vicariously by being deeply involved in another group member's experience.  These processes unfold over time and in relation to specific sequences of events.  Belinda, Scott, and Eleanor all learn from these experiences and apply their learning in specific ways.  However, there are key differences in the ways that these participants engaged with their peers' experiences, the content of their learning, and the impact of their learning.  I discuss these differences below.

*Ways of engaging with peers' experiences.*  Learning from others' experiences rests partially on how group members engage with those experiences.  These three vignettes illustrate at least three ways or "modes" of engaging with peers' experiences:  through empathy, through challenge, and through observation.

*Empathy.*  Belinda's vignette shows her engaging with Lynn's experience through empathy.  She frames her account of this experience with the words, "I remember going through that with her," indicating that she doesn't view herself as a mere observer, but as someone deeply connected to Lynn's experience and the events in Lynn's life.  She describes Lynn's emotional state around the time of these experiences ("angry and upset… frustrated") and uses language throughout that shows her attention to Lynn's changing disposition and her feelings about going through this transition ("it's really hard for me… She's definitely a much happier human being," etc.).  Although Belinda is describing events in Lynn's life, her genuine care and concern for Lynn and her emotional investment in Lynn's journey are palpable.

*Challenge.*  In the story that Scott tells, his primary way of engaging with Rebecca's experience is through challenge.  As he lays out the context for the story ("so we had a situation"), he paints her experience in stark terms: "people loved her stuff, but she was sitting there talking about all the things that went wrong."  He draws attention to Rebecca's reluctance and his frustration with her.  He describes confronting her and challenging her decision to give up "so easily," then challenging her place in the group.  Though his description makes him seem almost combative, he conveys that he cares about Rebecca's business and wants her to succeed at pursuing her passion.

*Observation.*  While Belinda and Scott both describe engaging with their peers' experiences in vivid, relational terms, Eleanor describes engaging with Tamara's experience in a more transactional mode.  Eleanor's attention is on Tamara's idea and its applicability in her own business.  She engages through observing as Tamara shares her idea for a guidebook with the group.  Eleanor recounts hearing about the development of the guidebook and having a light go off in her own mind.  She describes Tamara's experience in terms of the

steps Tamara took to develop the book.

     ***Content of learning.***  Learning from the experiences of others in the group takes

multiple forms.  The three vignettes vary in terms of the content of participants' learning as

well.  The stories illustrate the synthesis of new theories of effective action, the adaptation of

new business tactics, and the evolution of entrepreneurial identity.

     *New theories of effective action.*  Belinda indicated that Lynn's experiences taught her

to recognize what's not working as well as where she should be spending her time.  This is

how she understands the progression she witnessed Lynn going through as she decides to

close Tagsale.com down.  She also mentions learning "to see beyond what you're… focusing

on—and see other opportunities outside of it."  These articulations of her learning can be

described as general "rules" or theories for effective action.  They help Belinda conduct

herself and her business in new ways, leading to the identification of new opportunities (see

below).

     *New business tactics.*  From listening to Tamara's idea to develop a client guidebook,

Eleanor got the idea to adapt this tactic for use in her own business.  Not only does she adapt

Tamara's idea in a general sense, she also describes having observed the steps Tamara took

to develop her product, and seeing how she could take similar steps.  She realizes that she

can implement this idea as a way of addressing her clients' unmet needs in a new way.

     *Evolution of entrepreneurial identity.*  Scott and Eleanor each learn something

important about themselves as a result of what another individual in the group said or did.

Scott describes experiencing an "ah-ha moment" when he tells Rebecca, "I don't have a plan

B or C or D… This is it.  I have to make this successful."  Through this interaction he realizes that his mindset for dealing with challenges and his commitment to be successful

distinguish him from other would-be entrepreneurs who may not be as serious about success.

The experience solidifies his claim to entrepreneurial identity ("my business isn't a hobby")

and reinforces the notion that his work is his true passion.

Through the process of implementing her new business idea, Eleanor learns that she

can elevate the level of her work and be a more foundational resource for her clients. Her

words, "I really can do this," show how this realization changes her view of herself and what

she can accomplish through her work. She goes on to describe how these events enabled her

to envision herself helping her clients look at their businesses in a different way, and helping

to mitigate their pain. Later in the interview she puts this realization into context by sharing

with me about her vision as a person and how she has approached her business as an

expression of her purpose:

> My, um, vision as a person is to… be my brother's keeper in some ways, be my
> sister's keeper, um, be there to support human beings in whatever their path might be.
> Um, and I think I—that's when—when I started the business I tried to translate that
> into business terms, which was to be a guide and a support for the small business
> owner trying to grow the business and make a life for him or herself as well as
> supporting their employees in a healthy and positive way. So I think that that's my
> mission in life is to just be there, um, to support, and, um, and give whatever
> knowledge or information or wisdom that I may have gathered over 71 years to help
> someone, um, be successful.

Her comments indicate that what she learned from this experience in her coaching group has

significance beyond her business results. Doing more foundational work with clients and

helping to mitigate some of their pain connects her to her sense of purpose and enables her to

live her vision of being her sister's keeper in new ways.

*Impact of learning.* The primary impact of Scott's learning in this vignette are his

strengthened claims to entrepreneurial identity described above. The impact of Belinda and

Eleanor's learning is visible in the specific actions they took as a result of their experiences. Their actions help illustrate the impact of their learning on their lives and businesses. Belinda describes capitalizing on a new business opportunity, while Eleanor talks about developing new products.

*Capitalizing on a new opportunity.* According to Belinda, learning to recognize what's not working and where she needs to spend her time helped her identify and capitalize on an opportunity to partner with a real estate company as a showing agent. She recalls not making any money in her interior design business but also not wanting to become a full-fledged real estate agent even though it might be more lucrative. She realizes that her current situation isn't working and by "looking outside her box," identifies an opportunity to become a showing agent. This helps to expand her professional network while also exposing her to home buyers who could potentially be clients for her design business in the future.

*Developing new products.* As a result of Eleanor's learning about offering more foundational resources to her clients, she develops a guidebook to help small businesses deal with employee turnover. In addition to selling the book, she develops a set of tools from the book into separate standalone products sold on her website. In her words, "it was creating, you know, a couple of different products from one idea."

**Process moves related to learning vicariously.** Entrepreneurs learn different things in different ways when they engage vicariously in other group members' experiences. Participants' ways of engaging vicariously, coupled with the content or products of their learning, form three distinct but related process moves which all revolve around the notion of learning vicariously:

- Learning new theories of effective action by engaging empathetically in another group member's transition.

- Learning about one's entrepreneurial "self" by observing or challenging another group member's idea or decision.

- Learning new business tactics by observing another group member's idea.

As described above, the impact of these process moves on the lives and businesses of the participants varied as well. The primary impact of these processes included (a) strengthening claims to entrepreneurial identity, (b) capitalizing on a new opportunity, and (c) developing new products. The entrepreneurs in this study also learned through receiving and responding to different forms of feedback from their group members. In the next section I present three vignettes illustrating different processes of learning through feedback.

**Learning Through Feedback**

Entrepreneurs benefit in multiple ways from receiving feedback from other group members. The next three vignettes illustrate process moves related to learning and changing through direct feedback from other group members. They are participants' stories about receiving feedback from others in the group, learning from this exchange, and applying their learning in specific ways.

In the first vignette, Pierre receives feedback from his group that changes the way he thinks about his writing skills. In the second, Lynn talks about how the group grants her "permission" to reprioritize and what this means to her. In the third, a member of Rigsby's group shares an insight about her that fundamentally expands Rigsby's awareness of her own behavior.

### "Becoming" a Skilled Writer (Pierre)

Pierre's story below illustrates how consensus feedback from the group can challenge an individual's beliefs and assumptions. In this case, Pierre discusses how his coaching group's positive feedback shifted his beliefs about his own writing skills, which in turn allowed him to pursue a new business opportunity he wouldn't have otherwise thought himself prepared for.

> I'm kind of insecure about my writing, umm, because when I sit down to write something, umm, sometimes I can get into a flow, umm, but more often than not it's like pulling teeth. And I will spend forever, umm, trying to put the idea I have in my head, explain it the right way with words. And, umm, so I've always been kind of self-conscious that I—I don't write as well as—as the ideas come out and I'm a little frustrated with that.

> And through the process of the group we had to read, uhh, out loud to the other members certain assignments that Naomi had given us, umm, uhh, which involved, you know, a type of journaling or a type of essay on how you feel about this or that. And, umm, I was really surprised to find that other people responded in—when I read my statement that—that they related so well or they thought, "Wow, you really put that into words that I wouldn't have thought to do that that way, and that really resonated with me."

> And that felt amazing to me because I really felt like, you know, when it came time for that session where we all had to read our stuff that mine was just gonna be the most disjointed, not really cohesive bundle of, you know, umm, stream of consciousness.

> And, uhh, so it really, umm, it was—it was an area where I didn't feel like I had a strength, and through the group they were able to say, "No, you know, that is—that is a good element of, you know—keep working on that, keep doing that because you've got something there." Umm, which was great.

> And I think hearing that from the group was better than hearing it from the coach because the coach almost sometimes is like Mom, like you know your mom's gonna think you're great... I did feel like the group was more of a consensus, and so it wasn't like one person telling you, "Oh yeah, I think you're good at that," it was the whole group going, "Oh wow, that was a really good essay," whereas, you know—so that was really cool.

> And—and now with this—this new venture that I'm working on, it's absolutely

essential because I'm having to dictate lesson plans, I'm having to dictate procedure on a lot of stuff with this new company, and it's all gotta be written down in like a, you know, SOP kind of thing.  Umm, and a year ago or two years ago I would've been so uncomfortable with that.  Umm, but now it's—I'm able to put those ideas into a format and, umm, and get it out.

And then—and then you create a feedback loop, which is another new experience for me.  So, umm, in the past I'd been keeping all these ideas in my mind and I know that I'm losing some of them because, you know, you have that really inspirational moment, umm, late at night before you go to bed and if you don't write that down, as good as it is and you think you're going to remember it the following day, a lot of times you don't.  And so documenting all that stuff is a new regime for me as well.  And I'll come back and look at things and totally forget—it's almost like another person wrote it.  And I'm like, "Oh, I'm so glad that I wrote that down," because now I can take that concept which would've been lost and keep going.  So, umm, you know, it's, uhh, yeah, interesting tools.

E:  It's very interesting.  So when you—when you received that feedback from the group that, "No, you're—this is great.  This is great writing that you're doing—" how did that change the way you thought about yourself as an entrepreneur, as a business owner?  Or even just as a person?

P:  Umm, it—well—yeah.  It, uhh, it—it put an immediate gag order on the critic in my brain that was saying, "You shouldn't even—you shouldn't even bother doing this because you're not really that good at it."  Umm, so that shifted.  Umm, and, uhh, and it—it basically gave me the comfort to just start doing it more… so it—it, you know, I mean, uhh, ultimately it gave me more confidence, you know, umm, and, uhh, kind of inspired me to—to do more of that.

### Getting Permission (Lynn)

In this vignette, Lynn tells the story of a conversation that took place in her group a few months after she closed Tagsale.com down.  She discusses the moment when her coaching group granted her permission to establish a new set of priorities, and what honoring those priorities now means to her.

L:  Um, really the interest in the market shot up and skyrocketed.  And the moment that I watched a football ad for a similar company, um, I went, "You know what?  I think I'm in the wrong business." And I decided to go ahead and close it down, and not too long after that Facebook came out with a competing product as well.

Uh, I remember we were filling out our—our goal sheets and [Julie] was asking us what, you know… "Put down here, what do you want for the next three months? What do you want for the next six months? What do you want—what do you want overall? What is the thing?" And I'm sitting there thinking, "Gosh, I just—I really don't wanna write this list of, like, you know, editing the website and—I don't—I don't really—I'm not focused on this right now. The sun is out and it's gorgeous and I really—I want my kids to be my priority."

And [Julie is] like, "So do it," you know? And I'm like, "Wait a minute. I just got permission! I just got permission to go have fun." You know, it felt like I was, like, fit in this little box before where, like, you have to get these things done and then, like, well, you know, "I could streamline the summer and I could just hit work a couple days a week and keep the ball rolling but not just be engrossed in it. And I could travel and go to the pool and just, you know, live the life that we have built so that I can."

E:  Huh. Wow. That's pretty big.

L:  Yeah. [laughs] It was, it was. To, you know, just to realize that, you know, "This is life, this is the life we lead, this is how we grow it, this is the hours that we have to dedicate to it, this is the choices that we've made, but what do we want to be the priority?" And our kids are definitely that. So I take that role. So if somebody needs to, you know, be out of school or go to a doctor's appointment or whatever, yes, we're entrepreneurs and yes, I have tons of things to do every single day, but I will choose them over doing—building the business.

### Addicted to Change (Rigsby)

Rigsby's vignette begins with her description of having just come through a difficult and stressful period. She talks about "coming back into normal" after this time and looking for ways to learn from the experience. She receives some valuable insight from Wendy, one of her peers in the group, that fundamentally expands Rigsby's awareness of her own behavior.

R:  Um, so I went through, like, a real rut last summer, um, where I was just—it was a combination of health problems and stress and just feeling really burnt out.  Um, and so I took, like, two or three weeks off and just didn't do anything and was trying to, like, soul search and whatever and try—and, you know, and so last fall was really me kinda coming back into normal.  And—and the end of, you know, the fourth quarter was really, um, about realigning, figuring out why I got to that point, how can I do things that are gonna make it better, how can I be strong in the new year and kind of take some of these lessons and—and implement that.  And Wendy, who I don't know if you're meeting with, um, she's a counselor, she's a therapist.  And so, um, so she has a really cool perspective, you know, and so sometimes that therapy feel really comes from her.

And, so—um, so Julie was saying, "Well, maybe it's this, maybe it's this," and, uh, Wendy said, "I think that you're addicted to change."  And I was like, "What do you mean?"  Like I had never heard anyone say that before.  And she was like, "Well, you know, everything you've described, part of the reason it started was because you felt like you were in a rut, like you didn't feel challenged, you were kind of losing your motivation, maybe you felt overworked or whatever."  Um, she's like, "But then you moved your office in July and when you moved your office your mood kinda changed, you had something new to focus on, things were going differently."  And so she kind of went through this, like, play-by-play and I was like, "Holy shit.  Like, I think she's right."  You know?

And I've really, like, that happened maybe four months ago and I've thought about that a lot because when I think about how I am as a person, as a business owner, as an entrepreneur, um, in all the facets, you know, sitting on a board, other stuff that I do.  I really am, like—to me, I equate, um, being stagnant with just, like, boredom and, you know, um, just, like, hitting your head against a brick wall.  You know, and, um, so yeah.  So I think she's right that, you know, even if it's small things like, "Today I'm gonna take a half day," you know, "I'm just gonna finish up some things at the house and whatever," cool.  That—that's exciting to me because it's different than, "Oh, I gotta work all day in the office."  So that's really helped me to, um, kinda rethink the way that I do things and recognize the warning signs if I feel—if I'm sitting at the office and I start, like, checking Facebook or CNN or something, I'm like, "Just go home. You're done."

So—so things like that.  I mean, it's—that's—that was a really defining moment for me recently, um, because it's really changed the way I think about my schedule, my business, everything.

E:  Say a little bit more about that if you can.  Like how has it changed your—your schedule and the way you're thinking about things?

R:  Yeah, just, um, just recognizing the fact that—I love situations where I'm put in an unfamiliar territory or environment and then have to figure it out, right?  Um, I love that kind of stuff.  And so by her, like, bringing that to my focus and realizing that I'm like that, um, doing just randomly—like I got online the other day and just randomly bought plane tickets to go visit a friend, you know? And it's like—things like that, like, really kinda just reshape the way that I think about things and then I don't feel so stagnant or trapped.

You know, I guess "stagnant's" not the right word. Trapped. I don't ever wanna feel like I'm trapped, like I'm going through the motions, you know? Um, so yeah, the things with our business, um, we put a bid in on another agency to purchase, um, two weeks ago. We don't know yet if it's gonna go through, but that would be a huge change for our business. It would almost double our business. We might have to hire somebody else, contacting all those new clients, like, it sounds like a pain in the ass to some people, but to me it's like, cool, like that's new, it's different. You know, how—how are we going to deal with this?

E: Something to figure out.

R: Exactly, yeah. It's a curveball. So yeah. So that's been really, um, really profound for me in the last couple of—of months.

**Analysis.** All three of these vignettes illustrate processes of learning and change related to receiving feedback from other group members. As in the previous section, these processes unfold over time and in relation to specific sequences of events. Pierre, Lynn, and Rigsby all learn from their experiences and apply their learning in specific ways. The vignettes show subtle variation in terms of the types of feedback the participants received from their peers, the content of their learning, and the impact(s) of their learning. However, they are alike in their illustrations of how participants defer to the feedback of their peers— even when it conflicts with their own previously held assumptions. In the section below, I discuss the differences, the similarities, and the overarching process moves evident in these participants' stories.

*Types of feedback received.* Meaningful feedback from peers can take many forms. The three vignettes above illustrate at least three different types of feedback: acknowledging latent skills, legitimizing personal values, and distinguishing habitual behavior.

*Acknowledging latent skills.* Pierre's group responds to the work he does as part of a group writing assignment. Much to his surprise, the group acknowledges the resonance of his words and encourages him to keep writing. This stands in stark contrast to Pierre's habitual way of thinking about his writing, making this a meaningful and impactful moment for him. He recalls expecting his essay to come off as "disjointed" and "not really cohesive," and describes the group's positive feedback as "amazing" to him. The feedback highlights a set of skills that Pierre didn't know he possessed.

In Pierre's view, the fact that the feedback reflected the consensus of the group, rather than the opinions of a single group member or his coach ("your mom's gonna think you're great"), was very significant. The group's consensus holds more weight and greater validity in his mind. It makes the feedback more believable.

*Legitimizing personal values.* In Lynn's case, her coach (Julie) initiates the feedback, though elsewhere in the interview she indicates that the rest of the group supported Julie's message ("They were like, 'Well yeah, I mean, if you can, why not? Just enjoy it'"). The group's feedback helps her legitimize her desire to focus on her family (rather than business) for the summer. This is something she wants to do but feels unable to do until the group gives her "permission." The language Lynn chooses conveys the fact that her desire is rooted in her personal values about family ("What do we want to be the priority?" "I will choose them [the kids] over doing—building the business"). The feedback she receives from her group enables her to reprioritize in a way that honors these values.

*Distinguishing habitual behavior.* The feedback that Rigsby receives from Wendy helps her distinguish a behavioral pattern of which Rigsby was previously unaware. In this case it is feedback from one individual group member (not the whole group or the coach) that makes Rigsby aware of her "addiction" to change. Rigsby indicates that Wendy's

professional expertise as a therapist appears to inform her view. The feedback is important to

Rigsby because it helps place her past feelings and experiences in a new context. She

describes Wendy's feedback as a "play-by-play" of Rigsby's circumstances and changing

mood during the previous months.

*Content of learning.* As above, these vignettes show variation in terms of the content

of participants' learning. The stories demonstrate learning about new strengths or capacities,

achieving new clarity about priorities, and developing new self-awareness.

*New strengths or capacities.* Although Pierre's latent writing skills may not be new

(they are previously undiscovered), they translate into what Pierre experiences as a newfound

strength or capacity for writing. Pierre mentions, "It was an area where I didn't feel like I

had a strength." But the group's feedback convinces him to embrace his work as a writer and

develop it further ("keep working on that"). In other words, from this exchange Pierre learns

that he can write effectively, and that his capacity for writing is valued by his peers.

*New clarity about priorities.* Lynn's interaction with her group helps uncloak and

elevate personal values that for Lynn were already there but suppressed. As a result, she

realizes that she wants her kids (not her business) to be her highest priority over the summer.

The group's feedback gives her permission to embrace her new priorities. From a place of

newfound clarity, she comments that although she is an entrepreneur and has "tons of things

to do every single day," she will choose her kids over the business.

*New self-awareness.* Pierre, Lynn, and Rigsby each learn to see themselves in new

ways as a result of receiving feedback from their groups. Pierre learns that he's able to put

his ideas into writing effectively, which contradicts his previously held beliefs about himself.

Through the process of uncloaking and embracing her new priorities, Lynn learns that the role she wants to play for her family supersedes her obligation to the business. This new arrangement represents a challenge to her past assumptions about what was most important to her.

In response to Wendy's feedback, Rigsby fundamentally expands her awareness of her own behavior and what drives it. She describes how the experience caused her to realize that she needs stimulation in order to stay engaged with work. At the same time, this realization helped her understand why she feels burnt out or unmotivated when things become stagnant ("I equate… being stagnant with… boredom and, you know… hitting your head against a brick wall"). Rigsby indicates that she was not previously aware of these inclinations ("I had never heard anyone say that before"). In other words, Wendy's feedback helps her learn about a new facet of her professional identity.

***Impact of learning.*** Learning through feedback leads to effective action. The impact of participants' learning is visible in the specific actions they take as a result of their group coaching experiences. Their actions illuminate the impact of their learning on their lives and businesses. Pierre is led to pursue a new business opportunity and initiates a new practice of reflective writing in his daily life. Lynn changes her work schedule for the summer. Rigsby finds new ways to keep her work fresh and different. In addition, all three negotiate their entrepreneurial identity claims differently as a result of their learning. I discuss each of these areas in detail below.

*Pursuing a new business opportunity.* According to Pierre, learning about his strengths as a writer gave him the confidence he needed to pursue a new business venture in which writing plays a central role. He says, "I'm having to dictate lesson plans, I'm having to dictate procedure on a lot of stuff with this new company, and it's all gotta be written down."

He credits his group coaching experience with giving him the confidence to "put those ideas

into a format and… get it out." Ultimately, learning through feedback enabled him to silence

any self-criticism that in the past might've prevented him from engaging in these activities.

*Creating a reflective practice.* Pierre also talks about creating "a feedback loop" by

writing down his ideas at night before he goes to bed. In the past he would rely on his

memory to keep track of ideas, often forgetting them by the morning. His newfound

confidence in his writing abilities inspired him to document his ideas in writing so he can

come back to them to develop them later.

*Spending less time at work.* As a result of Lynn's learning about priorities, she

streamlines her work schedule for the summer in order to spend more time with her kids.

She reduces the number of days each week that she spends at work—working enough to

"keep the ball rolling" without becoming "engrossed in it." As a result, she is able to travel

with her kids, take them to the pool, and so on. Lynn says her reprioritization allows her to

"live the life that we have built so that I can [do these things]." Her comments suggest that

the group's feedback has ultimately helped her capitalize on the entrepreneurial lifestyle she

created—by taking advantage of the flexibility of her role.

*Approaching work in new ways.* As a result of her expanded self-awareness, Rigsby

begins to approach her work in new ways in order to keep it fresh and exciting. She

describes some of these changes as small, such as spontaneously working a half day and

taking the rest of the day off, or booking a flight to see a friend, and so on. Others have had

much broader implications for her business, such as putting a bid in on another agency.

Rigsby says, "It sounds like a pain in the ass to some people, but to me it's like, cool, like that's new, it's different." In addition, she mentions that after having her addiction to change

brought to her attention, she has learned to recognize and respond to the warning signs of

impending boredom. For instance, if she notices herself watching CNN or checking

Facebook at work, she knows that it's time to go home, rather than struggle through the rest

of the day.

*Negotiating claims to entrepreneurial identity.* The overarching progression of

Pierre's story involves Pierre changing the way he sees himself because of the feedback he

receives from the group. The group helps him see himself in a new way, and this leads him

toward different choices and new opportunities. As a result, he enacts his entrepreneurial

identity in new ways as well. By accepting a role in a new venture that relies heavily on his

writing skills, he expands his sense of who he is as an entrepreneur and what he is capable of.

This shift is illustrated by the significant changes to his self-narrative: "it put an immediate

gag order on the critic in my brain that was saying, 'You shouldn't even—you shouldn't even

bother doing this because you're not really that good at it.'"

Lynn's shifting claims to entrepreneurial identity revolve around her decision to enact

a new set of values and to subordinate others. The realization that she can reduce her role in

the family business for the summer without sacrificing her entrepreneurial inclination

entirely is itself an expansion in her understanding of what it means to be an entrepreneur.

Where previously, being an entrepreneur meant putting business ahead of everything else,

she narrates her identity differently after this group coaching experience: "Yes, we're

entrepreneurs... but I will choose them [her kids] over doing—building the business."

Finally, Rigsby's experience leads her to construct her entrepreneurial identity in a

way that includes her need to shake things up on a regular basis. She implies that her old assumptions about being a business owner prohibited her from acting spontaneously ("Oh, I gotta work all day in the office").  As a result of Wendy's feedback, she too has expanded her sense of what it means to be an entrepreneur so that it includes this important aspect of her professional identity ("I love situations where I'm put in an unfamiliar territory… I don't ever want to feel like I'm trapped, like I'm going through the motions").  In other words, Rigsby's sense of who she is as an entrepreneur includes and embraces her addiction to change.

*Deference to peer feedback.*  Although the circumstances differ, all three participants grant their peers in the group a level of power and authority that they are unable or unwilling to grant themselves.  Lynn is unable to reprioritize until her group gives her permission.  Pierre is unable to see himself as a skilled writer until his peers describe him this way.  Rigsby is unaware of her attraction to change and unable to embrace it until someone else in the group distinguishes it for her.  In each of these cases the participants subordinate their old assumptions about self and business and embrace new ways of framing their experiences.  This suggests that peer feedback in a group coaching environment can be a potent lever for change.

**Process moves related to learning from feedback.**  Entrepreneurs learn different things in different ways when receiving feedback from their fellow group members, but defer to their groups' feedback in similar ways.  The type of feedback given and the content or products of participants' learning combine to form distinct but related process moves which all revolve around the notion of learning through feedback:

- Developing new strengths or capacities through receiving feedback that acknowledges latent skills.

- Achieving new clarity about priorities through receiving feedback that legitimizes personal values.

- Acquiring new self-awareness through receiving feedback that helps distinguish habitual behaviors.

As described earlier, these moves impact the actions and entrepreneurial trajectories of the participants in multiple ways, including (a) pursuit of a new business opportunity, (b) creation of a reflective practice, (c) more time spent with family and less at work, (d) new ways of approaching work, and (e) new claims to entrepreneurial identity. One common theme across all three vignettes is that the participants granted power and authority to their peers in the group that they denied themselves. They deferred to their peers' feedback even when it conflicted with their previously held assumptions, suggesting that feedback from other members in a coaching group can be a potent lever for learning and change.

**Counter-Narratives**

Entrepreneurs do not always learn or change in meaningful ways as a result of their group coaching experiences. Contrary to the previous six vignettes, neither Mila nor Ted recalled learning or changing significantly as a result of their group coaching experiences. As stated above, Mila felt her group's focus on goals and accountability was a poor fit for her needs at the time. Ted, on the other hand, showed a strong attachment to his group and clearly found his experience of belonging meaningful. However, neither described experiencing learning or meaningful change as a result of their participation. In the vignettes below, Mila contrasts her group coaching experiences with another group she belongs to that better matches her needs, while Ted struggles to describe how he benefits from participating in his group.

### It's Just Not What I Needed (Mila)

M:  Well, before I got into the group with, um, Julie, me and Rigsby were in a group
of women of John Maxwell.  Well, one of our friends did John Maxwell books, so we
started to come together at every—for a couple of years we would do John Maxwells.
And we did it in a group book study.  Loved it.  We—because we could share
everything and stuff.  And then Rigsby told me that she was in the one with Julie.  I
think I've been with Julie maybe four or five and we got one more.  Not my cup of
tea.  I liked the book study thing a lot better…  Um, Julie's an awesome person and
I've known Julie for quite a bit and we've met work—at different events off and on.
Not my cup of tea.

Nothing against her.  It's just not my cup of tea.  Because we're only meeting once a
month and it's just not enough.

E:  You need something more—more frequent?

M:  At least once a week or something like that.  With the book study we were
meeting once a week.  Loved it.  We were going through the book, we read.  And
sometimes—I don't know if Rigsby mentioned, um, the book study, but sometimes
we get off target and we're checking in with each other's business.  So it was more
than us doing that book study.  So—so now we even still meet, uh, every two weeks
for breakfast because we've developed a friendship and we've developed
relationships, but we're steady checking in on businesses.  With the one what I'm
doing with Julie once a week, where are you at with your goals?

E:  Doesn't do it for you.

M:  Not doing it for me anymore.  Which is not a bad thing, because you don't know
that till you do it.  Whenever you decide to go into a group, you don't know until you
get to that group if this is gonna be the one for you or not.  Because I've done so many
different ones and I've done a lot of different goal-setting things and stuff like that, I
probably should've went a different way than to that.  I think that one would be better,
uh, for somebody—different levels, beginners.  Something like that, you know?

The point that I'm at now to get me to the next level I need the knowledge instead of
that one-on-one check-in.  Yeah, I'm looking for more knowledge.  So I think with
Julie's particular group, it's a good group, nice people in there.  It's just not what I
needed.

You gotta find a group that's gonna help you to get what you need, that—like my
girls, I call them my girls, when we do our book studies and things like that, we are

such a diverse group, all at different levels, all in different businesses, but we developed a common bond of friendship in there also where we're more supportive to each other than more, uh, business.

### The Only Takeaway (Ted)

E: Has [your participation in the coaching group] affected the way you think about your business?

T: It has affected the way I think about my business—only from the standpoint of that idea that I got from—the postcard idea [an idea for sending hand-written postcards to prospective clients]. That is the big one. That's the—that's the one that stands out. That's the defining one. And, um, that's really the only takeaway that I have.

E: That's fine.

T: Uh, that is the takeaway that I have. Because everything else is just—going back to the way I am, you know, you know, she'll, you know, Julie will write down on her whiteboard, you know, whatever the question is or whatever the goal is or whatever the—the deficiency is that we need to get better on, you know, and—and even though I'm verbalizing it and we're writing it down and we're taking notes, I mean, I know it. It's—it's—I didn't—I guess—I don't know if this is a pride thing, but I don't necessarily need this group to tell me that I have this deficiency or I excel in this area. But I guess what she's doing is she's bringing it to light so that others can keep you accountable, perhaps.

E: Yeah, that accountability piece, yeah. Huh. And do they? Do they hold you to account? Do they try? [laughs]

T: Actually, no. You know, I haven't had any conversations with any of them.

E: Huh. Okay.

**Analysis.** Mila and Ted describe their experiences in strikingly different terms than their counterparts. Mila indicates that she is not finding value in her coaching group and gives several reasons why. Ted dwells on his one takeaway—an idea he got from another group member which he hadn't yet implemented at the time of the interview due to financial constraints.

Interestingly, Mila goes on to describe her book study group in ways that closely echo what others have said about their coaching groups. Indeed, many of the same background conditions appear to be present in the book study group. She speaks about being able to "share everything" with the book study group (commonality) and develop close friendships with her fellow group members (cohesiveness). She mentions how the group checks in on each other's businesses (social support), and she implies that the group uses books and dialogue to engage with new knowledge and perspectives (exchange). This suggests that different types of groups can support meaningful learning for entrepreneurs if they share similar background conditions. In Mila's case, the book study group provided a level of knowledge and friendship that her coaching group hadn't at the time of the interview.

In Mila's estimation, focusing narrowly on goals and accountability may suit novice entrepreneurs better, although overall this study suggests that entrepreneurs at many levels of experience can and do find a structure of accountability to be an important factor in their meaningful experiences. Ted conveyed similar feelings about accountability in his group ("I haven't had any conversations with them") although elsewhere in the interview he refers to a time when Julie tracked him down on Facebook to follow up on actions he committed to.

Ted states that he doesn't need the group "to tell me that I have this deficiency or I excel in this area." Although he acknowledges that the coaching exercises Julie leads help him verbalize and write down goals and/or areas of "deficiency," he doesn't seem to find these activities meaningful. He assesses his experience in the group primarily from the perspective of business ideas and business leads. This sets up a conflict between the value he expects to find and the one aspect of the group that he actually does describe as meaningful: the experience of belonging with/to a group of peers. This conflict continues to play out in our interview (see Part 3 below) as I continue to press him on the question of how he benefits from his participation in the group.

**Conditions and Process Moves: A Tentative Connection**

Having discussed the process moves illustrated by participants' stories of meaningful group coaching experiences, I now turn to the relationship between the conditions described in Part 1 and the process moves described in Part 2. The data suggest there may be an important connection between these two different types of phenomena. The nature of their relationship is twofold.

First, individual member perceptions of background conditions appear to influence whether they experience opportunities for learning and change. For example, when a group member does not experience these conditions (even if others in the group may), she or he is unlikely to experience meaningful learning or change as a result of participating in group coaching. Such was the case for Mila, who described her coaching group as lacking the common bond of friendship and the relevant information that have made her book study group a more meaningful source of learning and change.

Second, the presence of particular background conditions doesn't on its own guarantee meaningful learning and change. Even for a member who does experience these conditions, such as Ted, learning and change may not take place. Despite the meaningful sense of belonging Ted experienced with his group, he struggled to recall any specific experiences which resulted in learning or change.

Mila and Ted's counter narratives suggest that additional factors (e.g., the group member's level of self-awareness, the degree of relevance of peers' experiences and feedback, etc.) may influence whether an individual learns from her or his experiences in group coaching. The conditions appear to set the stage, but do not automatically precipitate learning and change. Further research is needed to gain more insight into this relationship.

**Conclusion of Part 2**

The study revealed a range of possible process moves illustrated by participants' stories of their meaningful experiences in group coaching. The moves reflect individual and social processes of learning and change that unfold over time and through specific sequences of events. Two different categories of moves emerged from the data: those that demonstrate learning vicariously and those that demonstrate learning through feedback.

Participants' stories of learning vicariously varied across three dimensions: (a) their ways of engaging with peers' experiences, (b) the content of their learning, and (c) the impact of their learning. Three distinct process moves incorporating these elements are as follows:

- Learning new theories of effective action by engaging empathetically in another group member's transition.

- Learning about one's entrepreneurial "self" by observing or challenging another group member's idea or decision.

- Learning new business tactics by observing another group member's idea.

The impact(s) of these processes included (a) strengthening claims to entrepreneurial identity, (b) capitalizing on a new opportunity, and (c) developing new products.

Participants' stories of learning through feedback varied across three dimensions as well: (a) the types of feedback they received from their peers, (b) the content of their

learning, and (c) the impact of their learning.   However, the stories were alike in their

portrayal of participants' deference to the feedback of their peers.  In each case the

participants described examples of subordinating their old assumptions about self and

business and embracing new ways of framing their experiences, all as a result of receiving

feedback in their groups.  This suggests that peer feedback in group coaching can be a potent

lever for learning and change.  Three distinct process moves incorporating these elements are

as follows:

- Developing new strengths or capacities through receiving feedback that
  acknowledges latent skills.

- Achieving new clarity about priorities through receiving feedback that legitimizes
  personal values.

- Acquiring new self-awareness through receiving feedback that helps distinguish
  habitual behaviors.

The impact(s) of these processes included (a) pursuit of a new business opportunity, (b)

creation of a reflective practice, (c) more time spent with family and less at work, (d) new

ways of approaching work, and (e) new claims to entrepreneurial identity.

Furthermore, entrepreneurs do not always learn or change in meaningful ways as a

result of their group coaching experiences.  According to one counter-narrative in this study,

the background conditions for meaningful learning (commonality, cohesiveness, social

support, exchange) may be present in other types of groups, and finding the right fit with the

right group at the right time is paramount.  According to the other, coaching exercises or

activities that provide structure and/or aid in personal reflection may not always benefit group members in the way they are intended to.  In addition, participants' expectations about the value they will receive from group coaching may not be aligned with what they actually value most about their group coaching experiences.

The data also suggest (but are insufficient to conclude) that meaningful learning and change has the potential to occur for group members when the background conditions distinguished in Part 1 are perceived as being present.  Yet, the presence of the conditions alone doesn't necessarily guarantee meaningful learning and change.  Further research is required to better understand this relationship.  In Part 3 (of three) below, I present a series of vignettes illustrating the impact of the relational context of the interview itself on participants' constructions of their meaningful group coaching experiences.

## Part 3: Relational Context of the Interview

The meaning of past experiences continues to evolve through the course of the interview.  As stated in Chapter 3, individuals narrate or "perform" their experiences and their identities for specific audiences—in this case, the researcher.  As they look backward from the present and reflect on past experiences, participants reconstruct the meaning of past events in the present context of the interview.  These processes of reflection and reconstruction are important features of the social interaction between researcher and participant.  By turning the lens around on these interactions, it is possible to examine their impact on participants' meaning making and entrepreneurial identity development.

In Part 3 below I present a series of vignettes which illustrate the impact of the relational context of the interview itself on participants' meaning making.  I explore three types of exchanges between participant and interviewer: *negotiating belonging, co-creating successful entrepreneurship*, and *co-creating conscious learning*.  In each of these examples, the interaction between participant and interviewer influences the construction of events and their meaning.  These "discursive performances" highlight the co-constructed nature of narrative data and the influence of the research interview on participants' meaning making and learning.

## Discursive Performances

The following are three examples of speech acts or discursive performances through which participants came to view their experiences and/or themselves in new ways.  The first picks up with Ted at a point in the interview where my line of questioning leads him to assert a new identity claim.  In the second, Eleanor redefines herself as a successful entrepreneur.  In the third, Lynn becomes newly conscious of something she has been learning through her group coaching experiences.

**Negotiating belonging (Ted).**  At this point in my interview with Ted, he has described his initial skepticism about coaching, stemming from the fact that he already knows what he needs to do and doesn't need a coach to tell him.  The idea of using handwritten postcards to follow up with clients and referral sources is the one major takeaway he can name, but he hasn't actually implemented this practice.  Aside from this one idea, he seems to struggle to explain how his participation in the group has benefited him ("that's really the only takeaway that I have").  Despite these facts, he has spoken very clearly about his sense of belonging with his group and what that means to him.  As an interviewer, this apparent conflict between Ted's feelings of belonging and his inability to name any distinct benefit from his participation left me somewhat perplexed.  I began to wonder whether my interview with him was making him realize that he wasn't receiving much value or benefit from his coaching group.

As I pressed him more directly about other ideas he might have gotten from the group, or other significant events that might've happened, and so on, he still couldn't think of anything, and I noticed a shift in his demeanor. Perhaps he was frustrated with my questioning or embarrassed that his answers didn't seem to satisfy me. In any case, I began to feel awkward and somewhat frustrated by the interview. I struggled to reconcile Ted's enthusiasm for the group with what seemed like a lack of any significant or impactful benefit.

Things finally come to a head in this next section of our exchange when my blunt questioning appears to catch him off guard.

E: Do they hold you to account? Do they try? [laughs]

T: Actually, no. You know, I haven't had any conversations with any of them.

E: Huh. Okay.

T: Yeah.

E: Huh. So what do you get out of this?

T: [laughs] I don't know. Maybe I'm still new enough that I haven't really experienced the full effect. Maybe that's it. Because, like I said, the thing that defines my experience there is that idea, that business idea that I got out of it. And I got a client out of it. Um, and at this point—I mean, I think this will be—

[long pause]

You know what? I think I will find more value in this when this new business endeavor is off the ground. Because some of the things that are talked about in the group from other people would be, "How do I deal with this employee situation?" "How do I deal with this vendor situation?" and I haven't got there yet. I'm gonna get there because I am—got three people getting ready to come on board hopefully, once I get some more money, and those things will happen. So perhaps once I get into this a little bit deeper, then—then I'm gonna start finding more value in this type of—this type of service.

E:  Yeah. That makes total sense.

From this point forward, Ted begins to describe his relationship to his group in terms of the future instead of the past.  He talks about how he will benefit from other group members' experiences as his business grows and he encounters similar challenges of his own.

Taken at his word, Ted seems to be reflecting out loud on how his business needs to get to a certain point before he would derive value from the group.  However, narrative analysis involves "interrogating how talk among speakers is (dialogically) produced and performed as narrative" (Riessman, 2008, p. 105).  In addition to considering *what* is said, this involves asking *who* (or to whom speech acts are directed), *when*, and *why* (or for what purpose)?  From this perspective, a higher-order story of my exchange with Ted enters into view.

Ted's laughter and his long pause indicate that my questioning has caught him off guard—although this wasn't my intention.  Consequently, my questions about the value of the group might've occurred like a threat or challenge to his sense of belonging.  After all, Ted's earlier comments indicate that his experience of belonging to this group is very important to him.  If he can't offer a rationale for his participation in the group that seems to satisfy me (the interviewer), how can he claim legitimacy as a member of the group?  How can he argue that he truly belongs there?  How does this then contribute to the meaning produced through our exchange?  Ted's own words (described above), in combination with several contextual elements from the interview, seem to support this interpretation.

For example, the audio recording of my questions and Ted's answers during this part of the interview contains several pauses, awkward silences, and instances of nervous laughter.  These can be indications that either the participant or the interview (or in this case, both) are feeling uncomfortable. Our discomfort intensified while I continued to question Ted, and as it slowly became clearer that he wasn't able to point to any examples of significant learning or change. Though it is never said explicitly, all of these data taken together support as an explanation that Ted's sense of belonging or his legitimate belonging to the group is being challenged by our interaction.

Ted's mode of defense is to point to the business case for his participation in the group (the postcard idea, the one client referral, etc.), but this is rather thin. The long pause gives him time to abandon this tack and develop a new rationale—a new story about the value the group will hold for him in the future. At this point, he appears visibly relieved and sounds significantly more confident.

While this small shift in temporal focus seems very subtle, Ted's performance in this part of the interview is very important. Rather than allowing his interaction with me to convince him that the group holds little value, he grounds his rationale for participating in his aspirations for the future. He doubles down on the group, defends it, and defends his membership in the group. He states that as his new business idea takes off, the group will become more valuable to him as a resource for navigating new situations. My positive response to his comments ("That makes total sense") helps legitimize this new formulation, dialogically cementing Ted's claim to belonging.

An overt focus on the business case for Ted's participation in the group obscures the more profound performance taking place beneath the surface. In this performance, Ted negotiates his belonging (to the group) by reconstructing the group's value as a function of the future he desires. His articulation of this future amounts to an assertion of a new claim to entrepreneurial identity. He belongs in the group because of who he will be as an entrepreneur. The higher-order story of Ted's entire interview is about the experience of

belonging, how powerful it can be in a group like this, and how that power can also be

invisible to those who experience it.

**Co-creating successful entrepreneurship (Eleanor).** At an earlier point in the

interview, Eleanor talked about how she defines the word *entrepreneur*:

> Someone who has… a vision to see a need that needs to be addressed… and [who] can figure out a way to make that happen… to fill that niche… to reach out into the marketplace that has that need or that desire and, um, bring all of their creativity into addressing that need or that—or filling that niche.

Where this vignette begins, she is discussing the impact of an idea she adapted from another

group member's experience and implemented in her consulting practice. As we continue our

conversation, I ask her a question that inadvertently prompts her to construct her

entrepreneurial identity in a new way.

> Er: Huh. Wow, that's cool. That's very cool to see how that develops. Um, did that—thinking about that experience, uh, did it affect or change the way you saw yourself as an entrepreneur?

> El: Um, I think so. I think, um, you know, it was like, well, I could—you know, I really can do this. You know, I—I really can, um, do something other than just, um, coach my own clients, you know, in terms of, um, how they handle employee issues, um, or go in and do some transactional work for them or create their handbook or, um, you know, make responses to the unemployment claims that people are filing. I could do something that was, um, more foundational, um, something that they could use to really look at their business in a different way and, um, maybe head off some issues that, um, that they—if they had—they acknowledged to see that there were some of these issues in their future, there were ways they could handle them and, um, mitigate the—the pain that, you know, some of that can cause in the business.

> Er: Mm-hmm. Wow. So—so if you're doing that, if you're kind of proactively, um, putting out this content that helps people, um, mitigate, you know, uh, future problems in their business, what kind of entrepreneur does that make you?

> El: Successful? [laughs] I don't know. Well, um, you know, when we talked about my definition of—of entrepreneur, it's finding a problem and coming up with a creative solution to, um, address that problem. Well, then I would think that—that I would then fit my own definition.

In this example, the dialogue between participant and researcher produces a new identity claim for Eleanor—a claim to successful entrepreneurship. When I asked the question, "what kind of entrepreneur does that make you?" I had no idea what to expect. I just wanted to understand how Eleanor viewed herself in the context of the accomplishments she was describing. Her laughter in response to her own vocalization of the word "successful" conveys the newness of this claim and the tentative grasp with which it is held. Yet, she goes on to explain that by her own definition she is undeniably a successful entrepreneur.

In this case, Eleanor already had a definition of successful entrepreneurship in mind before our interview even began. What the interview process contributes to her meaning making is the co-construction of her identity *as* a successful entrepreneur. This connection that Eleanor makes in response to my line of questioning illustrates the influence of the participant-interviewer interaction on the construction of events and their meaning. Our conversation imparts Eleanor with a new sense of who she is as an entrepreneur.

**Co-creating conscious learning (Lynn).** In the example below, Lynn becomes consciously aware of her learning about holding on and letting go. At this point in our interview she had been talking about how the group helped her start Tagsale.com. She talks about the group's support and empathy throughout the ups and downs of establishing a business. I then ask her if the group's support through those times helped her learn anything from those experiences. I've traced this thread below through three different points in our conversation.

> E: Did that help you learn as an entrepreneur? So there's this—there's—in other words, you're talking about how it—it helped boost your confidence to do it, um, to sort of support you when you had, uh, challenging times or—or issues, they shared in

your anger, uh, they shared in your victories.  Did you learn from those experiences?

L:  I don't know that I necessarily learned from the experience in the group.  Um (p) simply because although we're getting together as a group, we have our own goal sheets in front of us.  You know, you're editing it as you go, you're—you're filling out your own dreams and your own, uh, game plan and your—you know, what am I gonna do in the next 30 days?  How am I gonna look at this situation differently?  And it's—and it's all independent.

[Conversation continues…]

L:  I mean, going back to the example of me deciding that I'm gonna embrace summertime.  I mean, that really was a huge—it was a huge shift for me because I was coming straight out of closing my business… I was—I wasn't feeling, um, at a loss, but I was still carrying the weight of being overwhelmed by two businesses.  So I wasn't giving myself the liberty of accepting that, "You know what?  You don't have to carry this burden anymore.  You can prioritize your children.  And then you can streamline your workload to where you can accomplish both because you're not—you're no longer overwhelmed.  You've… closed your online business, you are—you are just here for doing this marketing role and growing this family business which sustains you and raising kids.  And raising kids can be okay."

[Conversation continues…]

E:  So I'm wondering, it sounds like maybe, and I don't wanna, um, make a jump here that doesn't resonate with you, but it sounds like throughout those—those experiences with the group you're learning about how you hold onto things and then how to let them go.  Is that…?

L:  I think that's a really great way to condense it, yeah.

Like, things that I find very important to be a part of, there's no cut-off for me.  It's like I just—I wanna continually be a part of them.  And then something else adds on and then something else adds on.

Yeah.  Helping you keep your priorities lined out to where you don't lose yourself in the mix or forget about the things that you really wanna do.

A shift in Lynn's awareness occurs in this vignette when I propose that she has been learning about how she holds onto things and how to let them go.  Up until this point, she maintains that although the group is very supportive and has helped her through many difficult experiences, learning really isn't the point.  She emphasizes that group members tend to work individually on their own businesses and not each other's.  Elsewhere in the

interview she concedes that she has learned about how to use the group's connections to find

new resources outside of her network, but she doesn't seem to consciously recognize that she

is also learning about herself until we talk about it together.

Lynn confirms my understanding with her comments about having "no cut-off" and

using the group to help keep her from losing herself in the mix.  We then talk about her

experience explicitly in terms of learning about these aspects of herself.  In essence, we co-

create a moment of conscious learning through our exchange, in which Lynn begins to see

the group as helping her learn about holding on and how to let go.

**Conclusion of Part 3**

As the three examples above illustrate, the meaning of past experiences continues to

evolve through the course of the interview itself.  The social interaction between participant

and researcher influences the construction of past events and their meaning.  As participants

look back from the present and reflect on their experiences, they reconstruct the meaning of

past events in the present context of the interview.   In the process, they narrate their

experiences and their identities in new ways.  Presented in this section were three types of

discursive exchanges between participant and researcher: negotiating belonging, co-creating

successful entrepreneurship, and co-creating conscious learning.

## Conclusion of Chapter 4

This study explored the impact of group coaching as a setting for entrepreneurial

learning.  The research question was, *Given the impact of social processes on learning and*

*identity, what does it mean to entrepreneurs to navigate their learning-related challenges in the context of a coaching group?* The study revealed three different types of phenomena that were central to participants' storied descriptions of meaningful group coaching experiences. First, the participants described several conditions or background characteristics that were present in their coaching groups and that contributed to their meaningful experiences. Second, a range of possible process moves were reflected in participants' stories of meaningful or defining experiences in group coaching. Finally, the relational context of the interview itself contributed to participants' meaning making, directly influencing their constructions of past events and their meaning.

**Conditions**

The background conditions that participants described in connection with their meaningful group coaching experiences fell into three categories: (a) characteristics of the social environment of the group, (b) characteristics of the social processes at work in the group, and (c) characteristics of the coach's presence in the group. Characteristics of the social environment fit into two main categories: descriptions of cohesiveness and descriptions of commonality. Participants' comments related to cohesiveness had to do with their warm and caring relationships with other group members, their fondness for the group itself, and their sense of belonging. Comments related to commonality reflected their feelings that their peers share similar goals and challenges, that they share a common bond with their peers in the group, and that they are not alone.

Three types of social processes emerged from the interviews: social support, exchange, and accountability. Social support encompasses the idea that the group can be a source of personal and/or emotional support and encouragement for members. Exchange refers to a reciprocal interchange of ideas, information, and feedback. Accountability refers to the processes through which group members hold one another accountable for the actions

and/or goals to which they commit.  Finally, participants described the role and influence of

their coaches in terms of applying cognitive models or frameworks (Naomi), asking the right

questions (Susan), and managing accountability (Julie).  Table 4 below provides a summary

of these background conditions.

Table 4

*Background Conditions*

| Condition | Description |
| --- | --- |
| **Characteristics of the social environment** | |
| Cohesiveness | Warm and caring relationships with other group members, fondness for the group itself, sense of belonging. |
| Commonality | Feelings that their peers share similar goals and challenges, that they share a 'common bond' with their peers in the group, and that they are not alone. |
| **Characteristics of the social processes** | |
| Social support | The group can be a source of personal and/or emotional support and encouragement for members. |
| Exchange | A reciprocal interchange of ideas, information, and feedback. |
| Accountability | The processes through which group members hold one another accountable for the actions and/or goals to which they commit. |
| **Characteristics of the coach's presence** | |
| Applying cognitive models | Using various conceptual frames or lenses to introduce coaching activities and discussions in the group. |
| Asking the right questions | Asking questions that keep the discussion going and guide group members toward making their own conclusions. |
| Managing accountability | Following up on group members' goals and commitments, directing them toward actionable steps, holding them to account, etc. |

**Process Moves**

The study revealed a range of possible process moves illustrated by participants'
stories of their meaningful experiences in group coaching.  The moves reflect individual and
social processes of learning and change that unfold over time and through specific sequences
of events.  Two different categories of moves emerged from the data: those that demonstrate
learning vicariously and those that demonstrate learning through feedback.

Participants' stories of learning vicariously varied across three dimensions: their ways
of engaging with peers' experiences, the content of their learning, and the impact of their
learning.  Their stories of learning through feedback varied across three dimensions as well:
the types of feedback they received from their peers, the content of their learning, and the
impact of their learning.  However, all three stories of learning through feedback also shared
a common theme of deference to peer feedback.  These participants granted power and
authority to their peers in the group that they denied themselves.  They deferred to their
peers' feedback even when it conflicted with their previously held assumptions, suggesting
that feedback from other members in a coaching group can be a potent lever for learning and
change in entrepreneurs.  Table 5 below shows a typology of possible process moves and
their impact(s).

Table 5

*Typology of Process Moves*

| Type | Process Move | Impact(s) |
| --- | --- | --- |
| Learning vicariously | Learning new theories of effective action by engaging empathetically in another group member's transition. | Capitalizing on a new opportunity. |
| Learning vicariously | Learning about one's entrepreneurial "self" by observing or challenging another group member's idea or decision. | Strengthening claims to entrepreneurial identity. |
| Learning vicariously | Learning new business tactics by observing another group member's idea. | Developing new products. |
| Learning through feedback | Developing new strengths or capacities through receiving feedback that acknowledges latent skills. | Pursuit of a new business opportunity.<br><br>Creation of a reflective process.<br><br>New claims to entrepreneurial identity. |
| Learning through feedback | Achieving new clarity about priorities through receiving feedback that legitimizes personal values. | More time spent with family and less at work.<br><br>New claims to entrepreneurial identity. |
| Learning through feedback | Acquiring new self-awareness through receiving feedback that helps distinguish habitual behaviors. | New ways of approaching work.<br><br>New claims to entrepreneurial identity. |

Finally, entrepreneurs do not always learn or change in meaningful ways as a result of their group coaching experiences. Coaching exercises or activities that provide structure and aid in personal reflection may not always benefit group members in the way they are intended to. In addition, participants' expectations about the value they will receive from group coaching may not be aligned with what they actually value most about their group coaching experiences. For some entrepreneurs, similar background conditions (commonality, cohesiveness, social support, exchange) may be present in other types of groups, and finding the right fit with the right group at the right time is paramount.

**Relational Context of the Interview**

The meaning of past experiences continues to evolve through the course of the interview itself. The social interaction between participant and researcher influences the construction of past events and their meaning. As participants look back from the present and reflect on their experiences, they reconstruct the meaning of past events in the present context of the interview. In the process, they narrate their experiences and their identities in new ways. Presented in this section were three examples of meaningful discursive exchanges between participant and researcher: negotiating belonging, co-creating successful entrepreneurship, and co-creating conscious learning.

## CHAPTER FIVE: DISCUSSION

The purpose of this study was to explore the experience of group coaching as a setting for individual learning and change in entrepreneurs. The research question asked what it meant to entrepreneurs to navigate challenges related to EL and identity construction in the context of a coaching group. To answer this question, I conducted in-depth narrative interviews with eight entrepreneurs about their meaningful or "defining" moments in group coaching.

In Chapter 4, I discussed three types of phenomena reflected in their stories. The first were common conditions characteristic of the coaching groups and their activities. These included *cohesiveness, commonality, social support, exchange,* and *accountability,* as well as three characteristics of the coach's role in the group: *applying cognitive frameworks, asking the right questions,* and *managing accountability.*

The second type of phenomena were a range of process moves on the part of participants which depicted unfolding learning and change. These fell into the broad categories of moves that demonstrate *learning vicariously* and moves that demonstrate *learning through feedback.* The third type of phenomena were discursive performances illustrating the influence of the research experience itself on participants' constructions of past events and their meaning. I described three examples of meaningful exchanges between participant and researcher that impacted participants' meaning making: *negotiating belonging, co-creating successful entrepreneurship,* and *co-creating conscious learning.* In this chapter, I discuss the significance of these findings and explore the study's contributions to the entrepreneurship and coaching literatures. I also explore the implications of this research for future research and practice.

## Contributions to Literature

This study makes several contributions to the literature on coaching and EL. First, the results of this study show that group coaching can be a viable context for supporting entrepreneurial learning and change on multiple levels. This extends the knowledge base, answering Wang and Chugh's (2014) call for research that illuminates the various social contexts in which EL occurs. The study successfully applies EL theory to the new social context of group coaching, confirming several conclusions from past research and also addressing notable gaps.

Second, the study contributes to an understanding of *where* or *under what conditions* EL unfolds within group coaching. Participants in this study described seven common conditions or characteristics of the group coaching environment in connection with their meaningful experiences in group coaching. When present, these conditions support EL and entrepreneurial identity development. These findings shed light on the social environment and social processes that make group coaching conducive to EL. Many of these conditions are consistent with theory shown in the group psychotherapy literature (Foulkes, 1948, 1986; Yalom & Leszcz, 2005), which is not fully understood in the context of EL. This study begins to address this gap in the EL knowledge base.

Third, the study advances an understanding of *how* or *in what ways* participant entrepreneurs experience learning in this context. The stories participants told revealed a range of process moves illustrating learning and change through vicarious experience and direct feedback. While these results address Wang and Chugh's (2014) call for research that explores the social processes that support EL, the results also advance coaching knowledge by showing how group coaching can facilitate experiential learning in entrepreneurs, and by

further defining the subdiscipline of group coaching in relation to dyadic (one-on-one)

coaching.

Finally, this study shows that the research experience itself can be seen as an

extension or a continuation of the group coaching experience. Participants' stories are

constructed for the interview context in ways that support, develop, or transform the meaning

of past events. Their experiences are not necessarily fully processed and articulated in

advance. The interview conversation parallels the coaching process by providing what

Stelter et al. (2011) called, "space for the unfolding of narratives." I discuss each of these

four major contributions in detail below.

**Group Coaching Supports EL**

Group coaching is an effective context for supporting learning and change in

entrepreneurs. This study is the first to explore EL in a group coaching context and answers

Wang and Chugh's (2014) call for research that can help illuminate the social processes

involved in EL and the social contexts in which it occurs. Participants in this study described

a range of learning processes and outcomes in connection with their meaningful or defining

experiences in group coaching. Their stories were highly reflective of the experiential,

organizational, and social learning perspectives on EL discussed in Chapter 2, and support

several conclusions from past research in these areas.

**Learning from experience.** EL in a group coaching setting unfolds in relation to the

lived experiences of group members. This study confirms the work of past scholars who

described EL as highly experiential (Cope & Watts, 2000; Deakins & Freel, 1998; Higgins &

Aspinall, 2011). The learning pathways reflected in the participants' stories closely resembled  Kolb's (1984) cycle of experiential learning.  According to Kolb's theory, individuals engage with their concrete experiences through reflective observation, leading to the creation of new abstract concepts, which guide new actions and shape new experiences.

However, the participants' stories also reflect what may be their different learning styles.  A learning style is essentially an individual's preference for engaging in different phases of the learning cycle (A. Y. Kolb & Kolb, 2005).  For example, Eleanor's story about adapting Tamara's idea for her own business reflects the abstract conceptualization (AC) and active experimentation (AE) phases of the learning cycle, which are favored by people with a *convergent* learning style.  These individuals tend to excel at the practical application of new ideas and focus on technical rather than interpersonal tasks.

Belinda's story about engaging in Lynn's life transition reflects a preference for the concrete experience (CE) and reflective observation (RO) phases of the cycle.  Individuals who share these preferences are said to have a *divergent* learning style (A. Y. Kolb & Kolb, 2005), which is associated with emotionality, interest in people, and generating ideas in response to concrete situations.  Finally, Pierre's story about "becoming" a skilled writer depicts learning through *assimilation*, which involves reflective observation (RO) and abstract conceptualization (AC).  Individuals with an assimilating learning style tend to excel at putting new information into a logical form, and tend to gravitate toward ideas and abstract concepts.

Regardless of where they started the learning cycle, participants in this study repeatedly described navigating critical episodes or critical learning events in the context of their coaching groups, engaging in reflection and sense making, and taking different actions as a result.  In addition, their stories revealed that experiential learning in this context can involve complex social processes. Although several participants described instances which involved learning from their own critical episodes, others described learning vicariously from events experienced by others in their groups. While learning in this setting is highly experiential, it doesn't necessarily depend on one's own experience. Echoing Zhang and Hamilton's (2009) findings, EL can and does occur vicariously when group members engage deeply in the experiences of others in their group.

**Learning on multiple levels.** The entrepreneurs in this study told stories illustrating processes of both lower- and higher-level learning from experience, which is consistent with the organizational perspective on experiential learning discussed in Chapter 2 (Argyris & Schön, 1978; Burgoyne & Hodgson, 1983). Participants reported learning new business ideas and tactics (lower-level), as well as new theories of effective action (higher-level) and new ways of understanding or relating to entrepreneurial identity (higher-level). I anticipated that their stories would reflect lower-level (adaptive) learning, as entrepreneurs frequently become adept at such learning (Higgins & Aspinall, 2011). On top of this, past research has shown that peer groups provide exposure to new ideas and information (Brett et al., 2012), and I assumed the coaching orientation of the groups in this study would help ensure a developmental focus.

More surprising, however, were the many instances in which participants engaged in exploratory (higher-level) learning. Such learning involves reflecting critically on one's values and assumptions, and searching for and discovering new solutions (Wang & Chugh, 2014). Burgoyne and Hodgson (1983) wrote that entrepreneurs rarely engage in experiences that lead to higher-level learning. However, they must learn to reflect critically in order for their firms to survive and grow (Higgins & Aspinall, 2011). Many of the entrepreneurs in this study described situations in which their coaching groups helped them to reflect critically

on their thoughts, feelings, experiences, and assumptions. In these cases, the participants

learned new ways of viewing their situations and themselves, and took new actions as a

result.

These results are important, given Shane and Venkataraman's (2000) call for research

that contributes to an understanding of how entrepreneurs develop the skills and resources

needed for exploratory learning. This study suggests that group coaching can help

entrepreneurs develop these skills and resources by (a) introducing new information and

perspectives that stimulate critical reflection, (b) creating a supportive atmosphere that

nurtures introspection and insight, and (c) providing encouraging feedback from peers that

can legitimize new insight and self-knowledge. These components are analogous to

Mezirow's process of transformative learning (Mezirow, 1991).

The study also addresses Wang and Chugh's (2014) related questions about what and

how entrepreneurs engage in "unlearning" (the intentional discarding of practices). The

participants in this study most notably engaged in unlearning about themselves. In other

words, by critically reflecting on their assumptions about their entrepreneurial selves, several

of the participants deconstructed their past notions about who they were and what they were

capable of, which in turn led to new constructions of entrepreneurial identity. As above, this

process is consistent with the notion of transformative learning described by Mezirow

(1991). This type of learning is comparatively rare, which suggests that group coaching can

be a valuable developmental setting for entrepreneurs.

**Learning with and from other entrepreneurs.** In a group coaching context,

learning is a highly social phenomenon. This study found that entrepreneurs learn with and from their peers in the coaching group by exchanging ideas, information, and feedback; and by vicariously engaging in each other's experiences. In some cases these social processes led to the acquisition of practical knowledge, while in others they stimulated critical reflection that led to higher-level learning. These findings confirm the outcomes of past research on entrepreneurial peer learning (EPL).

Previous studies of EPL, for example, have found that critical reflection is enhanced by exposure to alternative perspectives (Zhang & Hamilton, 2009) and questioning about individuals' behaviors and assumptions (Florén, 2003). Entrepreneurial peer networks can be a source of specialized knowledge and can foster the exchange of new ideas (Brett et al., 2012; Kuhn & Galloway, 2015). As mentioned above, learning can also be triggered by external events, such as the experiences of peers (Zhang & Hamilton, 2009). This study extends the knowledge base to the social context of group coaching, showing that group coaching can be an effective context for supporting EPL.

It is important to note, however, that in order for this learning to occur, certain conditions must be present in a group. In the section below, I discuss these conditions and their connections to the literature on group psychotherapy.

**Conditions Needed to Achieve EL**

This study contributes to an understanding of *where* or under what conditions EL unfolds in a group coaching context. It revealed that certain characteristics of the social environment of the group, the social processes at work in the group, and the coach's presence in the group, create an environment that supports EL and entrepreneurial identity development. Many of the conditions identified are consistent with theory shown in the group psychotherapy literature (Foulkes, 1948, 1986; Yalom & Leszcz, 2005) and adapted by group coaching scholars (Kets de Vries, 2011, 2014; Thornton, 2010).  Similar concepts have

been explored by researchers of EL (Brett et al., 2012; Cope, 2005; Florén, 2003; Kuhn et al.,

2016; Zhang & Hamilton, 2009) and entrepreneurship education (Pittaway, Matlay, &

Edwards, 2012; Preedy & Jones, 2017), however group psychotherapeutic theory has not

been fully explored in these contexts.  This study begins to address that gap.

**Cohesiveness and commonality.**  For example, participants in this study highlighted

the roles of *cohesiveness* and *commonality* in shaping their meaningful experiences that led

to learning.  As stated in Chapter 2, *group cohesiveness* is one of several group

psychotherapeutic factors identified by Yalom and Leszcz (2005).  It refers to "the attraction

that members have for their group and for the other members" (p. 75).  Kets de Vries (2014)

noted that the state of connectedness and belonging associated with group cohesiveness acts

as a major catalyst for change.  Fusco et al. (2015), who studied group coaching for senior

organizational leaders, referred to group cohesion as "the bedrock upon which all further

individual and group work was to take place" (p. 137).  The current study suggests that group

cohesiveness can be a catalyst for entrepreneurial learning and identity development as well.

Past EL research has shown that social bonding and friendship play a key role in

supporting social learning among students of entrepreneurship (Preedy & Jones, 2017); and

that long-term, stable peer groups help members overcome their competitive mentalities and

form strong relationships that foster information sharing (Zhang & Hamilton, 2009).

Furthermore, the close relationships that form through group work promote group social

processes that may serve as a foundation for individual learning (Preedy & Jones, 2017).

This study confirms these findings and suggests that such relationships bridge the divide

between business and personal support.  In addition, this study shows that these friendships and caring relationships can develop and support learning despite some group members' considerable reluctance and/or skepticism (initially) about joining a peer group.

Likewise, the condition of *commonality* described in Chapter 4 closely resembles the psychotherapeutic factor of *universality* (Yalom & Leszcz, 2005) mentioned in Chapter 2. Past research has shown that peer learning networks or groups can help entrepreneurs overcome barriers to learning by reducing their isolation. This happens precisely because entrepreneurs share the same types of challenges and can relate to one another's experiences (Kuhn et al., 2016; Zhang & Hamilton, 2009). The present study supports these findings and suggests that the rich personal connections group members form with one another over time contribute to a sense of commonality or a common bond.

**Social support and exchange.** The conditions of *social support* and *exchange* discussed in Chapter 4 closely resemble the psychotherapeutic mechanisms of *holding* (Winnicott, 1971) and *exchange* (Foulkes, 1948, 1986) outlined in Chapter 2. As Thornton (2010) explained, these two mechanisms facilitate learning and change in a group coaching setting. Sufficient levels of safety and trust (holding) allow group members to engage openly with difference and the unknown (exchange). EL researchers have acknowledged that EL is a social phenomenon (Cope, 2005) and that entrepreneurs often learn from their peers (Taylor & Thorpe, 2004). Social learning has also been described as an important aspect of entrepreneurship education (Pittaway et al., 2012). However, social interaction with peers can also provide a source of emotional support, nurturing, and/or encouragement (Preedy & Jones, 2017).

Participants in this study explained that the emotional support and encouragement they received from their groups allowed them to view group coaching as a resource for support and helpful information, rather than as an evaluative, critical, or competitive environment. This safe and encouraging atmosphere led to a reciprocal interchange of ideas, information, and feedback (exchange) between group members. This kind of exchange of ideas, perspectives, and information among trusted peers has been discussed previously by Collins et al. (2006), Brett et al. (2012), and Zhang and Hamilton (2009).

Together, these findings support the views of Thornton (2010) and Kets de Vries (2011, 2014) that group psychotherapeutic theory is especially pertinent to the study and practice of group coaching. However, the study adds to their views by showing that these same psychotherapeutic mechanisms also help facilitate experiences that lead to both lower- and higher-level learning in entrepreneurs. This helps illuminate the relationship between group psychotherapeutic theory and EL, and establishes this relationship as a potential focus for future EL research. For example, group psychotherapeutic theory may help explain why entrepreneurs learn in certain types of group environments and not in others (Zhang & Hamilton, 2009). Moving forward, a group psychotherapeutic lens can help researchers identify and further explore the complex social processes that facilitate learning and change in entrepreneurs.

**Different coaching approaches, similar group conditions.** Finally, similar background conditions were found in connection with participants' meaningful group coaching experiences regardless of which groups they belonged to. As discussed in Chapter 4, the conditions were present despite the coaches' apparent differences in coaching style/approach. This shows that certain properties of groups or "group-ness" have an impact on learning beyond the effects of the coaching itself. In other words, when the right conditions are present, coaching is enhanced by the presence of a peer group in ways that are simply not available in a dyadic coaching environment. In the following section, I discuss this study's contributions to knowledge about *how* or *in what ways* entrepreneurs experience learning in a group coaching context. I place these findings in relation to the literatures on coaching and EL.

**Different Processes of Learning and Change**

This study advances an understanding of *how* or *in what ways* entrepreneurs experience learning in a group coaching context. Group members navigate different processes of learning and change, which unfold over time and in relation to specific sequences of events. In this study, two overarching types of process moves characterized learning in this context: learning from feedback and learning vicariously. Both types led to a variety of learning content and outcomes described in detail in Chapter 4. These findings contribute to emergent conversations in the entrepreneurship and coaching literatures. I discuss these contributions below.

**Emergent conversations in entrepreneurship.** As mentioned in Chapter 2 above, much EL research has focused exclusively on individual cognition, while the social processes and contexts that contribute to an individual's learning are often ignored (Fayolle et al., 2014; Wang & Chugh, 2014). The process moves outlined in Chapter 4 shed light on the social processes that facilitate learning in a group coaching context. In particular, these findings help address Wang and Chugh's (2014) questions about what and how entrepreneurs learn from the successes and failures of other entrepreneurs, and how entrepreneurs acquire and integrate external information through the learning process. In addition, these findings contribute to the literature's emerging thread on identity formation and identity work in

entrepreneurship (Leitch & Harrison, 2016).

***Learning from others' successes and failures.*** Vicarious experience is known to be

a rich source of learning and personal growth (Holmes & Kivlighan, 2000; Kets de Vries,

2014; Thornton, 2010). In the context of entrepreneurship, Zhang and Hamilton (2009)

found that opportunities to observe or reflect on others' experiences contribute to the value of

peer learning groups. They suggested that peer learning may lower the costs associated with

experiential learning by allowing peers to learn from the mistakes and failures of others.

This study supports these conclusions, and helps identify what and how entrepreneurs learn

from others' successes and failures in a group coaching setting.

First, this study shows that engaging vicariously in others' successes and failures can

result in both lower- and higher-level learning, as described in Chapter 4. Examples include

learning new business tactics, learning new theories of effective action, and learning about

one's entrepreneurial "self." In Eleanor's case, another group member's success at

implementing a new business tactic led Eleanor to adapt the tactic for use in her own

business (lower-level learning). Later on, she describes how this experience leads her to

develop multiple new products. Ultimately, this makes her work with clients deeper and

more fulfilling, and changes how she sees herself as an entrepreneur (higher-level learning).

Her example shows that what entrepreneurs learn vicariously from other group members'

experiences may begin as lower-level learning, but may continue to unfold over time in ways

that lead to higher-level learning and identity development.

Second, in addition to explaining *what* participants learned by engaging vicariously in

other group members' successes and failures, this study highlights *how* they learned from these experiences. As outlined in Chapter 4, participants engaged with their peers' experiences in three distinct ways: through empathy, through observation, and through challenge. These could be described as representing the concrete experience phase of Kolb's (1984) experiential learning model, except that the experiences originate with events taking place in the lives of other group members.

As participants engaged with their peers' experiences, however, these experiences became shared; they became the participants' experiences as well. This is evidenced by Scott's story about challenging Rebecca after her failure to pursue the entrepreneurial opportunity the group helped her create. His reaction to her experience became an important moment in his own entrepreneurial development. In essence, Rebecca's story became Scott's story, too. In summary, group coaching fosters learning vicariously from the successes and failures of other group members. The content of this learning varies, but can be either lower- or higher-level, and learning that begins as lower-level may lead to higher-level learning over time. In addition, the successes and failures of individual group members can become shared experiences for the group, leading to secondary (vicarious) learning and change in other group members.

***Acquiring and integrating external information.*** As discussed in Chapter 4, Wang and Chugh (2014) drew a distinction between *sensing* (external) and *intuitive* (internal) learning, calling on researchers to explore the roles of each and the social processes that support them. One question they posed is how entrepreneurs search for and acquire external information, and how they make sense of this information through the learning process. As illustrated above, vicarious experience is one channel through which group members acquire external information in a group coaching setting. Such information can take the form of new ideas or business tactics, for example, which can be adapted to fit a new business situation or context. Over time, adaptive learning of this nature can lead to higher-level intuitive learning, as it did for Eleanor when her success at implementing a new business idea eventually changed the way she thought of herself as an entrepreneur.

However, learning through feedback, as represented by this study, intertwines the roles of sensing and intuitive learning. The feedback that participants received could be considered a form of external information taken in through the senses, but it wasn't always information about the external business environment. In some cases, what they heard from their peers were observations about their own internal or personal intuitive worlds.

For example, Rigsby learned from Wendy's observations that she (Rigsby) is addicted to change. As indicated in Chapter 4, participants deferred to these socially constructed observations more or less as facts, assimilating them in ways that led to meaningful learning and change on multiple levels. For Rigsby, the external information led to intuitive learning. This learning changed how she understood herself as an entrepreneur and created a new possibility of approaching work in ways that were more consistent with her entrepreneurial identity.

Rigsby's example shows how the roles of sensing and intuitive learning become more complex in a group coaching environment. What is external to one individual can still be internal to the larger group, particularly when sufficient levels of safety and cohesiveness support a collective spirit of inquiry. In other words, although Rigsby received external information from Wendy, the learning process was still collectively intuitive. Likewise, what the group senses about an individual may stimulate an intuitive process for the individual. Such was the case for Pierre, whose group's observations about his writing triggered a huge shift in awareness for him that led to the pursuit of a new business opportunity. These examples, though limited by sample size and specific to these particular coaching groups, help illuminate the roles of sensing and intuitive learning, and the social processes that support them in this context.

***Entrepreneurial identity construction and maintenance.*** As discussed in Chapter 2, EL involves more than the acquisition of knowledge. It also involves the construction and maintenance of entrepreneurial identity (Higgins & Aspinall, 2011). The study of entrepreneurial identity is not entirely new. However, most existing research adopts an essentialist orientation, which views identity as a relatively static and objectively definable phenomenon (Leitch & Harrison, 2016). Leitch and Harrison advocated for more research that recognizes entrepreneurial identity as dynamic and fluid, and that explores the processes through which entrepreneurial identities are constructed and negotiated. This process-oriented view emphasizes the "temporally and contextually constrained domain of identity creation" (p. 187).

The process moves outlined in Chapter 4 support Leitch and Harrison's (2016) view and begin to address this gap in the literature. First, these findings tell retrospective and descriptive stories of entrepreneurial identity construction-in-motion. In several cases, participants' learning from their group coaching experiences resulted in the creation of new claims to entrepreneurial identity. For example, Pierre claimed his strength as a writer and used it to pursue a new business opportunity. Eleanor *became* a successful entrepreneur by creating products that made her work fundamentally more satisfying. Rigsby claimed and integrated her addiction to change—an aspect of her personality that had previously been unconscious and in conflict with her entrepreneurship.

Second, it is interesting to note that despite their relevance and applicability to an

entrepreneurial context, not all of these constructions reflect a hegemonic "discourse of

enterprise" as described by Mallett and Wapshott (2015). Instead, group members drew from

a variety of discursive resources to construct and alter their entrepreneurial identities in

relation to the specific situations that arose in their groups. This supports Watson's (2009)

view that identity work is relational and dialogic, and that entrepreneurs use multiple

discursive resources in multiple ways to make sense of what happens in their businesses, and

to negotiate their identity claims with others.

Third, this study describes the processes through which entrepreneurs in a group

coaching context negotiate and maintain changes in entrepreneurial identity. In essence,

group members negotiate changes to their identities through their action and behavior

consistent with Sveningsson and Alvesson's notion of identity work (2003). In each of the

examples above, the participants enacted their changed identities through subsequent changes

to their business activities. Whether pursuing new opportunities, launching new products, or

injecting spontaneity into tired routines, group members performed these new aspects of their

identities outside of group meetings and within their businesses. Within their groups, the

accountability-holding condition of the social environment promotes reporting back after

action and helps ensure that group members do actually enact these changes. Scott's story

about Rebecca indicates that entrepreneurial identity negotiation fails in the group when

group members fail to stay the course of action or fail to enact their changed identities in

ways their groups consider legitimate.

To summarize, this study answers Leitch and Harrison's (2016) call for research that

explores the processes involved in entrepreneurial identity construction and maintenance.

The process moves detailed in Chapter Four illustrate identity construction-in-motion within a group coaching context. Participants' identity constructions pulled from a variety of discursive resources, rather than from one hegemonic and all-encompassing enterprise discourse. The moves also demonstrate how entrepreneurial identity claims are negotiated in the coaching group through action and social interaction with group members. In the next section, I discuss how the process moves identified in this study contribute to emergent conversations in coaching research.

**Emergent conversations in coaching research.** The process moves described in Chapter 4 contribute to the coaching literature in three main ways. First, they help illustrate how group coaching facilitates experiential learning and identity construction in entrepreneurs. Research on group coaching is limited (Stelter, 2012; Van Dyke, 2012), and researchers have given much more attention to the study of organizational team coaching than to other types of unaffiliated coaching groups. This study is the first to explore unaffiliated group coaching in an entrepreneurial context, and to demonstrate the viability of group coaching as a platform for supporting EL and entrepreneurial identity construction.

Second, these findings contribute to an ongoing debate in the literature as to whether single-day or short-term interventions such as those studied by Barrett (2006), Kets de Vries (2005, 2011, 2014), and Ward (2008), should actually be considered group coaching. Although intervention styles such as these promote quick results or "change in a single session" (Ward, 2008, p. 73), others have defined group coaching as something that specifically happens over time. Thornton (2010), for example, stated that a multi-session format is necessary in order to reinforce and build on previous learning through continued reflection. Brown and Grant (2010) also stressed the iterative nature of "idea development and refinement" through multiple sessions (p. 41), and Stelter et al. (2011) noted that engaging in multiple sessions over time helped participants develop durable social networks with their peers in the group.

This study builds on the latter, long-term perspective. It supports the idea that multiple sessions over time allow for certain experiential and social learning processes to unfold that cannot possibly unfold in a single session. This is not to say that change can't happen in a single session. Indeed, several of the participants in this study experienced sudden changes in perspective within specific coaching sessions. Many of these were the coaching moments they remembered most vividly and recounted through their stories.

However, these moments were often the culmination of experiential processes that began much earlier, such as Lynn's founding and eventual closing down of her business, or Rigsby's period of intense burnout. These experiences happened over time and involved recursive sequences of action, reflection, and meaning making supported by the coaching group. They were aided by warm and caring relationships with other group members, which were also developed over time and through shared experience.

In essence, this study supports an understanding of group coaching as an experiential and recursively organized phenomenon that allows for (a) the unfolding of experience over time and (b) the revisiting of experience and its meaning by group members. In this setting, learning and meaning making also unfold and evolve over time (as illustrated in Chapter 4), in some cases even transcending the boundaries of the coaching relationship, as noted by Eleanor and Pierre. This supports Spence's (2017, October) view that the "sleeper effects" (or cumulative learning effects) of coaching may continue after the coaching relationship has ended. The study helps establish a foundation for continued research in this area.

Third, the process moves described in Chapter 4 help to further distinguish the subdiscipline of group coaching relative to dyadic (one-on-one) coaching. Knowledge of group coaching continues to lag despite recent growth in the number of theoretical works and empirical studies on dyadic (one-on-one) coaching (Grant, 2009, May; Passmore & Fillery-Travis, 2011). At issue are the distinctions that make group coaching uniquely itself. In other words, what distinguishes group coaching from dyadic coaching, other than the fact that it happens in a group?

In answer to this question, this study shows that a number of social processes support or enhance coaching in this context. Most importantly, participants' meaningful experiences in group coaching almost exclusively involved learning from peer feedback or learning vicariously by engaging in peers' experiences. In other words, these defining moments stemmed from group members' interactions with each other, as opposed to their interactions with their coaches alone. This again underlines the appropriateness of using group psychotherapeutic theory (Holmes & Kivlighan, 2000; Yalom & Leszcz, 2005) as a lens for the study of group coaching, and builds on the work of Kets de Vries (2014) and Thornton (2010) in this vein. In short, group coaching provides wider opportunities for reflection and exchange, and allows for more direct and less threatening feedback between individuals who are relatively equal in power (Thornton, 2010).

To summarize, the process moves outlined in this study make three main contributions to the coaching literature. First, they address a gap in the coaching literature by helping to illustrate how group coaching facilitates experiential learning and identity construction in entrepreneurs. Second, they support a long-term view of group coaching (Stelter et al., 2011; Thornton, 2010) in which experiential and social learning processes unfold over time and across multiple coaching sessions. Third, they help to further define the

subdiscipline of group coaching in relation to dyadic (one-on-one) coaching by highlighting

important mechanisms of learning and change that are specific to groups (Kets de Vries,

2014; Thornton, 2010). In the next section, I discuss findings related to the recursive nature

of the interview experience itself.

**The Research Process as a Continuation of the Coaching Experience**

Finally, this study suggests that the research experience itself can be seen as part of

the coaching experience—a continuation or culmination of the meaning-making processes

that begin in group coaching. As shown in Chapter 4, the meaning of group members' past

experiences continued to evolve through the course of their interviews. Participants reflected

on their experiences and reconstructed the meaning of past events for the present context.

These constructions were inevitably influenced by the interaction between narrator and

researcher, as all narratives are fundamentally co-constructed between narrator and audience

(Salmon & Riessman, 2008). In this sense, the interview conversations paralleled the

coaching process by providing what Stelter et al. (2011) called, "space for the unfolding of

narratives."

Instead of being fully formed already, the meaning of past group coaching

experiences *found* new form through the dialogic and performative processes inherent in

narrative interviewing (Riessman, 2008). In other words, most participants' meaningful

experiences weren't sitting ready and well-defined, their meaning fully processed and

articulated. In most cases, some additional conversation needed to occur in order for these

experiences to take shape in ways that sustained their developmental power.

Importantly, these conversations can be viewed as part of the participants' group coaching experiences—and as an extension or continuation of the meaning-making processes that began with the unfolding of actual events. These things really happened, but part of their developmental potency lies in their narration or re-narration in a new context. As Polkinghorne (1988) and others have argued, narratives lend meaning to human experience. This study shows that narrative about (and learning from) group coaching experiences continues to evolve over time and through subsequent dialogic inquiry.

These conclusions are consistent with Stelter's (2012, 2014) model of *third-generation coaching*, which emphasizes a collaborative partnership between coach and client, the purpose of which is to promote reflection, generate meaning, and invent new narratives that impact on identity and self-concept. However, this study extends the context of third-generation coaching by including the research interview itself as a continuation of the coaching process. This notion of *the coaching interview* (mentioned above in Chapter 3) presents rich opportunities for future research. Narrative interviewing could itself be considered its own type of coaching interaction, either in concert with or independent of group coaching, with important implications for practice.

This idea is not entirely new. White and Epston (1990) pioneered the application of narrative principles in family therapy. More recently, Drake (2007, 2014), Stelter (2009), and Vogel (2012) have each explored narrative approaches to coaching practice. However, there is some debate as to whether the goal of narrative practice should be to help clients externalize and re-author their "problem" narratives or to simply raise their awareness of how and what stories shape their perception of reality (Vogel, 2012). The coaching interview, as it is conceptualized above, leans toward the latter position, while also allowing for what Drake (2007) described as the client's development of a more evolved narrative repertoire.

The conceptual basis for these explorations into the influence of the research experience itself lies in an expanding notion of the role of reflexivity in research. In most interpretive research, reflexivity is dealt with by acknowledging the researcher's biases and assumptions that may affect the research project and its conclusions. However, as stated in Chapter 3, issues of reflexivity in this study go beyond the usual treatment. Here, they also include cultivating awareness of and attention to the reciprocal social interaction between researcher and participant, as well as the influence of that interaction on the investigative process and its results (Steier, 1991).

Viewed through this lens, there is a reflexive quality inherent in the relationship between the content of an interview about group coaching and what may be viewed as the parallel process of the interview itself. Steier (1995) referred to this phenomenon as "mutual mirroring," which is the idea that the researcher's communication processes and/or relationships may come to mirror and be mirrored by those that he or she is engaged in studying. The interviews in this study, for example, *may* have helped open reflective spaces for participants' experiences precisely because, from the participants' point of view, the interview process invoked or echoed the coaching relationship. Therefore, reflexivity can also be about acknowledging or even fostering these parallel processes that may emerge between content and process. By positioning these phenomena within the domain of inquiry, this study contributes to an evolving understanding of the nature of reflexivity in research.

In summary, this study makes several contributions to the literature on coaching and EL. First, the results of this study show that group coaching is a viable context for supporting entrepreneurial learning and change on multiple levels. Second, the study contributes to an understanding of *where* or *under what conditions* EL unfolds. Third, the study advances an understanding of *how* or *in what ways* entrepreneurs experience learning

in this context. And finally, this study shows that the research experience itself can be seen

as an extension or a continuation of the group coaching experience. In the next sections

below, I discuss the study's limitations, recommendations for future research, and

implications for practice.

## Limitations

Even with careful planning, all research studies have their limitations. Some

limitations are inherent to particular methods or modes of inquiry, while others may be

specific to the present research context. One limitation of this study is its small sample size.

Although the purpose of narrative research is to explore the particularities of a given context,

rather than to generalize to a broader population (Creswell, 2009; Josselson & Lieblich,

2003), the sample in this study was limited by access. Group coaching for entrepreneurs is

still a new phenomenon. Finding willing participants who met the study criteria was

extremely challenging. A larger sample might have strengthened the study by allowing for a

greater diversity of experiences and more robustly supported themes.

Another limitation involved the small number of groups studied and the distribution

of group members across these groups. Again, due to challenges with access, this study

included only four distinct coaching groups run by three different coaches. Given the wide

variation in group coaching practices from one program to the next, choosing group members

from across a wider range of groups might have made their similarities and differences more

apparent. Additionally, six of the eight participants in this study were coached by the same

coach even though they belonged to two different groups. A more even distribution of individuals to groups to coaches could have been achieved by interviewing one individual from each of eight different groups run by eight different coaches, or two individuals from each of four run by four, and so on.

This study took a single interview, narrative-retrospective approach to exploring entrepreneurs' experiences in group coaching. While this design produced rich and detailed stories of lived experience, it did not allow me to observe participants' changing experiences, perspectives, or attitudes as they evolved over time. A longitudinal component would strengthen the study, were it to be repeated. Multiple interviews at different stages of the group coaching journey, for example, might reveal different factors or patterns of learning and change, as well as any variability that might shape these factors and patterns over time.

Finally, as discussed in Chapter 3, interpretive research is subject to implicit bias (Creswell, 2009). This study is no exception. My own experiences as a coach, and specifically as a coach who regularly coaches groups of entrepreneurs, enters into both the study design and my interpretations of the data. My biases about the effectiveness of group coaching as an intervention for entrepreneurs, about what constitutes effective coaching and consultation, and so on, played a role in guiding my curiosity in the interview setting and in data analysis. In line with these personal beliefs and assumptions, I intentionally took an appreciative view of group coaching by exploring the social processes that *support* EL and entrepreneurial identity, versus the social processes that disrupt or obstruct learning. This does not detract from the importance of this study's findings. However, it does make evident the need for future research that could add to this study by exploring these other social processes.

## Recommendations for Future Research

As this study is the first to explore the intersection of group coaching and entrepreneurial learning, it establishes a groundwork for additional research in both of these areas. In the following paragraphs, I suggest several avenues for future entrepreneurship and coaching research based on the conclusions outlined above.

### Entrepreneurship Research

First, repetition of this study is necessary in order to confirm these findings. In particular, studies that involve larger sample sizes and a diversity of group coaching settings may help strengthen the claims made in this study. In addition, the dual methods of analysis (thematic and narrative) employed above are especially suited to studying these phenomena and could provide a useful framework for future researchers.

Second, this study helps to establish group psychotherapeutic theory as an appropriate lens for exploring EL in group settings. Moving forward, a group psychotherapeutic lens can help researchers identify and further explore the complex social processes that facilitate learning and change in entrepreneurs. In addition, given that the presence of the specific conditions described above only sets the stage for EL and doesn't guarantee it, what other factors are involved in supporting learning?

Third, the roles of sensing (external) and intuitive (internal) learning were explored in this study, but the findings suggest that the social processes involved in *learning through feedback* intertwine them and distort their boundaries in complex ways. For example, what is external to one individual can still be internal to the larger group, and what the group collectively senses may stimulate an intuitive process for one or more individuals. Simply put, internal and external, as descriptors of learning types, acquire additional nuance and complexity in groups. Further research is needed to better understand the interaction *between* these learning types in group settings where peer feedback is viewed as a mechanism of learning and change.

Another opportunity for entrepreneurship research lies in further exploration of the process of entrepreneurial identity negotiation in group settings such as group coaching. In this study, group members negotiated changes to their identities through their action and behavior both in and out of the group. The accountability structure of the coaching group seemed to support this process, while failure to enact new identity claims appeared to compromise their legitimacy in the eyes of other group members. Further research is needed to better understand these dynamics. How do individual entrepreneurs negotiate their evolving identities in the context of a dedicated peer learning (or coaching) group, and what social mechanisms support or inhibit this process? How and to what extent does the social mechanism of accountability support or inhibit the negotiation of entrepreneurial identity?

**Coaching Research**

Coaching researchers have only recently begun to explore the possibilities of group coaching, so the opportunities for future research in this area are vast. More research is needed, for example, in order to find out (a) how coaches are already using work with groups to enhance their practices, (b) how members of these groups experience their participation and its impact, and (c) what mechanisms of learning and change (including and/or beyond those explored in this study) help shape group members' experiences.

In particular, future research should aim to cultivate a more complete understanding of coaching in unaffiliated group settings, given the potential of this modality for fostering learning and change. For example, what populations, situations, or specific problem constellations stand to benefit most from this type of intervention? In what ways do they benefit (or not)? Also, what approaches, techniques, and/or theoretical perspectives are most relevant and important to practice in this setting? How, if at all, do these differ from coaching in organizations, work teams, or dyadic settings?

As discussed above, this study supports an understanding of group coaching as an experiential and recursively organized phenomenon which allows for (a) the unfolding of experience over time and (b) the revisiting of experience and its meaning by group members. Given that this is so, an opportunity exists for researchers who would study the unfolding and/or evolving effects of group coaching over time. In other words, if learning might not be "fully hatched" in the group, how can coaches support this process and encourage further hatching? Is learning from group coaching ever fully hatched? Or, does it constantly evolve through its own ongoing narration in various relationships and settings?

In addition, if learning in group coaching is viewed recursively, then presumably it benefits from additional "stirring." In other words, learning in this context appears to unfold through somewhat recursive arcs that are sustained by ongoing dialogic inquiry. If this is true, how can group coaches intentionally support these learning processes in an ongoing way? What form can and do these recursive arcs take both in and out of the group setting? What other dialogic contexts can support the evolving narratives of group members?

## Implications for Practice

Having reviewed contributions to theory and recommendations for future research, I

now turn toward implications for practice. This study offers several practical insights for

coaches, and some for entrepreneurs as well.

**Coaching**

First, a psychological perspective was highly useful for interpreting and

understanding participants' group coaching experiences. This suggests that coaches who

wish to practice in the group domain would do well to familiarize themselves with the

literatures on group counseling and group psychotherapy. Group counseling also deals with

the group as a context for learning and problem-solving. Unlike most group psychotherapy,

counseling groups tend to focus on conscious problems and short-term issues rather than

severe psychological problems (Corey, Corey, & Corey, 2010). However, as discussed

above, the group psychotherapy knowledge base also includes a rich and illuminating array

of resources for learning to work in unaffiliated group settings. These include Yalom and

Leszcz' (2005) ideas on group psychotherapeutic factors, and Winnicott's (1971) notion of

the holding environment. Coaching educators and others involved in coach training and

education should also consider incorporating these resources into their curriculum designs

where group coaching is concerned.

Second, my sense about the purpose and potential of group coaching aligns with

Stelter's (2012, 2014) view. The role of the group coach includes collaborating with group

members to promote critical reflection, meaning generation, and the invention of new

narratives that impact on identity and self-concept. Part of this process involves helping

group members reflect on and make sense of their learning over time. Some might argue that

not everyone needs help to fully process their learning. However, this study suggests that at least some people do, and that group members' learning may continue to unfold or evolve over time and through further dialogic inquiry.

In fact, a related implication for coaches is that a long-term view of the group coaching process seems appropriate for supporting this unfolding of learning over time. Practitioners may wish to design their group coaching programs in ways that allow for revisiting and supporting learning and its evolution. At the very least, group coaching should encompass multiple learning cycles such as those D. A. Kolb (1984) describes, including the phases of action in the world, concrete experience resulting from action, reflection on experience, and conceptualization that leads to further action. Shorter-term interventions may not allow for the same richness of learning and identity development that longer ones do. In addition, this study suggests that coaches should strive to revisit the meaning of past experiences through recursive exchanges that engage group members' collective resources for meaning making. In other words, they should revisit learning in the group in ways that lead to new collective understandings of an individual's experience and identity.

Others might argue that what appears to be an unfolding of learning over time may actually be a kind of performance aimed at negotiating one's identity with a new audience. However, these perspectives are not mutually exclusive. As this study shows, when individuals narrate their identities for new audiences, their understanding of the meaning of past events can change and/or evolve, resulting in new forms of conceptualization. In this way, the processes of identity negotiation and learning are intimately connected. The important point for coaches is that group coaching holds the potential to foster these interrelated processes.

A final implication for coaches concerns the influence of the research experience itself on participants' constructions of past events and their meaning. As discussed above, the research experience could be viewed as part of the coaching experience—a continuation or culmination of the meaning-making processes that begin in group coaching. This is in part due to the ability of narrative interviewing to help group members process their learning from their meaningful experiences in the group. This supports the notion of "the coaching interview" discussed in Chapter 3 and suggests that this type of interview could potentially constitute its own type of coaching interaction.

In other words, coaches may wish to consider incorporating narrative interviewing techniques into their group coaching programs—perhaps as an adjunct or complementary service. Doing so could help support the experiential, social, and recursive learning processes stimulated by clients' meaningful experiences in the group. The interview format can help clients explore and further conceptualize the meaning of these experiences, contributing to further learning and identity development.

**Entrepreneurship**

Two further practical implications concern entrepreneurs. First, this study demonstrates that group coaching can be a valuable resource for learning and development in entrepreneurs. In short, group coaching works and holds great potential. Those engaged in entrepreneurial paths may wish to consider participating in a group coaching program in order to more effectively respond to the distinct challenges of entrepreneurship.

By helping group members learn (and learn to learn) from their experience, overcome isolation, and develop their entrepreneurial identities, group coaching can contribute greatly to their entrepreneurial trajectories. Those who do choose to explore group coaching need to take into consideration the variability of group coaching approaches. This study suggests that longer-term programs with a focus on facilitating higher-level learning may be of greater value to entrepreneurs than other types of programs.

Second, this study reveals something about the nature of group coaching that for some may be counterintuitive. Namely, the most profound effects of participating in this type of group have less to do with obtaining specific advice or "nuggets" from the coach, and more to do with the social processes involved in simply talking through various challenges in a safe and supportive peer group. In other words, the informational content of a group coaching program doesn't always deliver the most meaningful results. Instead, it's the social interaction between group members, the special bond of shared experience, and the spirit of collective inquiry that can make group coaching such a meaningful platform for learning and development. This may run counter to some individuals' expectations about the kinds of programs that would benefit them. However, group coaching appears capable of contributing in ways that run contrary to implicit knowledge or expectation.

## Conclusion

The purpose of this narrative inquiry was to examine the impact of group coaching as a setting for individual learning and change in entrepreneurs. The study explored eight individual entrepreneurs' experiences bringing issues and challenges that they might otherwise engage with in isolation into a group coaching setting—a phenomenon I have defined as "coming in from the cold." It is the first study to investigate the intersection of group coaching and entrepreneurship, and as such, it advances scholars' understanding of the social processes that shape entrepreneurial learning and identity construction in a group

coaching context.

The study showed that group coaching is a viable platform for supporting

entrepreneurial learning and change on multiple levels.  In addition, it contributed to an

understanding of *where* or *under what conditions* EL unfolds, and *how* or *in what ways*

entrepreneurs experience learning in this context.  Finally, the study demonstrated that the

research experience itself can be seen as an extension or a continuation of the group coaching

experience.

Rich, detailed stories of lived experience undergird these findings, stories that at once

reveal the moving fabric of entrepreneurial lives and the social and historical contexts in

which these lives are embedded.  At their heart, these stories are tales of coming in from the

cold.  However, they are also stories about acquiring the resources to navigate successfully

once back out *in* the cold.  Fortified by shared experience and a sense of belonging,

broadened by an exchange of knowledge and ideas, and elevated through ongoing learning

about self and business, the protagonists in these stories find new expression in their

entrepreneurship and in the world.